Thomson Round Hall Nutshells

Criminal Law

UNITED KINGDOM

Sweet & Maxwell Ltd
London

AUSTRALIA

Law Book Co. Ltd
Sydney

CANADA AND THE USA

Carswell
Toronto

NEW ZEALAND

Brookers
Wellington

SINGAPORE AND MALAYSIA

Sweet and Maxwell
Singapore and Kuala Lumpur

Round Hall Nutshells

Criminal Law

Cecilia Ní Choileáin
BA (NUI), LL.B (NUI),
LL.M (TCD), BL (King's Inns)

SERIES EDITOR
Bruce Carolan

DUBLIN
THOMSON ROUND HALL
2006

Published in 2006 by
Thomson Round Hall Ltd
43 Fitzwilliam Place
Dublin 2
Ireland

Typeset by
Carrigboy Typesetting Services, County Cork

Printed by
ColourBooks, Dublin

ISBN 1-85800-453-5

A catalogue record for this book
is available from the British Library.

All rights reserved. No part of this publication may be reproduced or transmitted in any form or by any means, including photocopying and recording, without the permission of the publisher. Such written permission must also be obtained before any part of this publication is stored in a retrieval system of any nature.

©
Thomson Round Hall
2006

"Do mo theaghlach, Betty agus Seán Cathal,
agus do John, le meas, míle buíochas agus grá."

Acknowledgments

There are a number of people to whom I owe a debt of gratitude for helping with this book. I'd like to thank John Tully for helping with the typing. I'd also like to thank Catherine Dolan and Una McCann of Thomson Round Hall and David McCartney, formerly of Thomson Round Hall. A particular word of thanks goes to Susan Rossney, whose courtesy and patience have been exceptional. My thanks also go to my friends and colleagues: Jeanne Finlay BL, Katrina Preston BL, Majella Walsh BL and Ger Hussey BL, Harry Connolly BL, Niall Neligan BL, Dr Neil Maddox BL and Dr Steven Carruthers. Finally, I'd like to thank my friends and family.

Cecilia Ní Choileáin BA (NUI), LL.B (NUI), LL.M (TCD), BL (King's Inns) is a barrister and formerly a lecturer in the Department of Legal Studies, DIT.

Table of Contents

Acknowledgments vi
Table of Contents vii
Table of Legislation xvii
Table of Cases xix

1. INTRODUCTION 1
   1.1 The Function of the Criminal Law 1

2. SOURCES OF CRIMINAL LAW 3
   2.1 Statute 3
   2.2 Common Law 3
   2.3 The impact of Bunreacht na hÉireann 1937 4
   2.4 The European Convention on
       Human Rights (ECHR) 8
   2.5 The European Convention on
       Human Rights Act 2003 8

3. JURISDICTION OF THE IRISH COURTS IN CRIMINAL MATTERS 9
   3.1 The District Court 9
   3.2 The Circuit Court 10
   3.3 The High Court/The Central Criminal Court 10
   3.4 The Special Criminal Court 11
   3.5 The Court of Criminal Appeal 11
   3.6 The Supreme Court 13

4. ARREST AND DETENTION 14
   4.1 Arrest 14
   4.2 Rights on Arrest and During Detention 15
   4.3 Habeas Corpus 16

5. BAIL 17
   5.1 Jurisdiction to Grant Bail 17
   5.2 Valid Grounds for Refusal of Bail 18
   5.3 The Bail Act 1997 21
   5.4 Refusal of Bail—s.2 of the Bail Act 1997 21
   5.5 Sentencing 22
   5.6 Hearsay Evidence 23

6. TYPES OF PUNISHMENT 24
   6.1 Imprisonment 24
   6.2 Fines 25
   6.3 Community Service Orders 25
   6.4 Forfeiture 25
   6.5 Probation 26
   6.6 Compensation 26

7. THE ELEMENTS OF A CRIMINAL OFFENCE 27
   7.1 The Burden of Proof 27
   7.2 The Standard of Proof 27
   7.3 The *Actus Reus* 28
       7.3.1 State of Affairs 28
       7.3.2 Omission 29
       7.3.3 Voluntariness 30
   7.4 The *Mens Rea* 30
       7.4.1 Intention 30
       7.4.2 Direct Intention 30
       7.4.3 Oblique Intention 30
       7.4.4 The Presumption of Intent 32
       7.4.5 Recklessness 33
       7.4.6 Criminal Negligence 34
   7.5 Coincidence of *Actus Reus* and *Mens Rea* 35
       7.5.1 The *actus reus* and *mens rea* must coincide 35
       7.5.2 Continuing Act 35
       7.5.3 Duty 36
       7.5.4 The "Supposed Corpse Rule" 36
       7.5.5 Causation 36
   7.6 *Novus Actus Interveniens* 37
       7.6.1 The Eggshell Skull Rule 38

8. CRIMINAL LIABILITY 39
   8.1 Secondary Participation 39
       8.1.1 Aiding 40
       8.1.2 Abetting 40
       8.1.3 Counselling 40
       8.1.4 Procuring 41
       8.1.5 *Actus Reus* of Secondary Participation 41
       8.1.6 *Mens Rea* of Secondary Participation 41

8.2 The Doctrine of Common Design (Joint Enterprise) 42
    8.2.1 Withdrawal from Complicity 44
8.3 Vicarious Liability 44
8.4 Strict Liability 44
8.5 Absolute Liability 45
8.6 Criminal Liability of Corporations 45
8.7 Transferred Intent 46

9. HOMICIDE 47
   9.1 Murder 47
       9.1.1 Causation 48
       9.1.2 Attempted Murder 48
       9.1.3 Penalty on Conviction 48
       9.1.4 Aggravated Murder 48
   9.2 Manslaughter 49
       9.2.1 Voluntary Manslaughter 49
       9.2.2 Involuntary Manslaughter 49
       9.2.3 A Criminal and Dangerous Act 49
       9.2.4 Criminal Negligence 50
       9.2.5 Breach of Duty 50
       9.2.6 Penalty on conviction 51
   9.3 Infanticide 51
       9.3.1 Penalty on conviction 51
   9.4 Euthanasia 52

10. SEXUAL OFFENCES 53
    10.1 Rape 54
         10.1.1 Consent 54
         10.1.2 Vitiating Factors 55
         10.1.3 Submission 55
         10.1.4 *Mens Rea* 56
         10.1.5 Recklessness 56
         10.1.6 Penalty on conviction 56
    10.2 Rape and Murder s.4 of the Criminal Law (Rape)
         (Amendment) Act 1990 57
         10.2.1 Penalty on Conviction 57
    10.3 Sexual Assault 57
         10.3.1 Penalty on Conviction 58
    10.4 Aggravated Sexual Assault 58
         10.4.1 Penalty on Conviction 59

10.5 Statutory Rape 59
    10.5.1 Penalty on Conviction 60
10.6 Sexual Offences Against Mentally Ill Persons 60
    10.6.1 Defences 61
10.7 Offences Between Males 61
    10.7.1 Penalty on Conviction 61
10.8 Gross Indecency 62
    10.8.1 Penalty on Conviction 62
10.9 Incest 62
    10.9.1 Incest by a Male 62
    10.9.2 Incest by a Female 62
10.10 The Sex Offenders Act 2001 63

11. NON-FATAL OFFENCES 64
    11.1 Assault 64
        11.1.1 Consent 64
        11.1.2 Words as a form of assault 65
        11.1.3 Force 65
        11.1.4 Immediacy 65
        11.1.5 Punishment on Conviction 65
    11.2 Assault Causing Harm 65
        11.2.1 Punishment on Conviction 66
    11.3 Causing Serious Harm 66
        11.3.1 Consent 66
        11.3.2 Punishment on Conviction 67
    11.4 Threats to Kill or Cause Serious Harm 67
        11.4.1 Punishment on Conviction 67
    11.5 Syringe Offences 68
    11.6 Syringe Attacks 68
        11.6.1 Punishment on Conviction 68
        11.6.2 Spraying blood or a blood-like substance 69
        11.6.3 Punishment on Conviction 69
        11.6.4 Transferred Intent 69
        11.6.5 Stabbing with a Contaminated Syringe 69
        11.6.6 Punishment on Conviction 70
        11.6.7 Possession and Abandonment of Syringes 70
        11.6.8 Punishment on Conviction 70
        11.6.9 Punishment on Conviction 71
    11.7 Coercion 71
        11.7.1 Punishment on Conviction 71

11.8 Harassment 71
    11.8.1 Punishment on Conviction 72
11.9 Demands for Payment 72
    11.9.1 Punishment on Conviction 72
11.10 Poisoning 72
    11.10.1 Punishment on Conviction 73
11.11 Endangerment 73
    11.11.1 Punishment on Conviction 73
11.12 False Imprisonment 73
    11.12.1 Punishment on Conviction 74
11.13 Child Abduction 74
    11.13.1 Punishment on Conviction 74

12. OFFENCES AGAINST PROPERTY 75
    12.1 The Criminal Damage Act 1991 75
        12.1.1 Lawful Excuse 75
    12.2 Damaging Property. 75
    12.3 Damaging Property with Intent to Endanger Life 76
    12.4 Damaging Property with Intent to Defraud 76
    12.5 Arson. 77
        12.5.1 Punishment on conviction 77
    12.6 Threats to Damage Property 77
        12.6.1 Punishment on conviction 77
    12.7 Possession with Intent to Damage Property 78
        12.7.1 Punishment on conviction 78
    12.8 Unauthorised Accessing of Data. 78
        12.8.1 Punishment on conviction 78
    12.9 Theft and Dishonesty. 78
        12.9.1 The Criminal Justice (Theft and
               Fraud Offences) Act 2001 78
        12.9.2 Theft. 79
        12.9.3 Dishonesty 79
        12.9.4 Consent. 79
        12.9.5 Property 80
        12.9.6 Punishment on conviction 80
        12.9.7 Making Gain or Causing Loss by Deception . . . 80
        12.9.8 Punishment on conviction 80
        12.9.9 Unlawful Use of a Computer 81
        12.9.10 Punishment on conviction 81
        12.9.11 False Accounting 81

12.10 Burglary.................................... 81
   12.10.1 Trespass 82
   12.10.2 Entry................................. 82
   12.10.3 Punishment on conviction 82
12.11 Aggravated Burglary........................... 82
   12.11.1 Weapon............................... 82
   12.11.2 Punishment on conviction 83
12.12 Robbery..................................... 83
   12.12.1 Punishment on conviction 84
12.13 Handling 84
   12.13.1 Punishment on conviction 84
12.14 Possession of Stolen Property..................... 84
   12.14.1 Punishment on conviction 85

13. PUBLIC ORDER OFFENCES............................. 86
   13.1 The Criminal Justice (Public Order) Act 1994........ 86
   13.2 Intoxication in a Public Place..................... 86
      13.2.1 Punishment on conviction................... 86
   13.3 Disorderly Conduct in a Public Place............... 86
      13.3.1 Offensive Conduct....................... 87
      13.3.2 Punishment on conviction.................. 87
   13.4 Threatening, Abusive or Insulting Behaviour......... 87
      13.4.1 Breach of the Peace...................... 87
      13.4.2 Punishment on conviction.................. 88
   13.5 Obscene Displays 88
      13.5.1 Obscenity............................... 88
      13.5.2 Punishment on conviction.................. 88
   13.6 Wilful Obstruction 88
      13.6.1 Punishment on conviction.................. 89
   13.7 Enforcement of the Act.......................... 89
      13.7.1 Punishment on conviction.................. 89
   13.8 Riot.. 89
      13.8.1 Punishment on conviction.................. 90
   13.9 Violent Disorder 90
      13.9.1 Punishment on conviction.................. 90
   13.10 Affray 91
      13.10.1 Punishment on conviction................. 91
   13.11 Assault with Intent 91
      13.11.1 Punishment on conviction................. 92
   13.12 Assault or Obstruction of a Garda.................. 92

        13.12.1 Punishment on conviction 93
        13.12.2 Punishment on conviction 93

14. OFFENCES AGAINST THE STATE 94
    14.1 Treason 94
    14.2 Sedition 94
    14.3 The Official Secrets Act 1963 95
    14.4 The Offences Against the State Acts 1939–1998 96
        14.4.1 Section 18 96
        14.4.2 Section 19 97
        14.4.3 Section 20 97
        14.4.4 Section 52 98
        14.4.5 The Offences Against the State
               (Amendment) Act 1972 98
        14.4.6 Section 3 98
        14.4.7 The Offences Against the State
               (Amendment) Act 1998 99
        14.4.8 Section 2 99
        14.4.9 Section 6 99
        14.4.10 Section 10 100

15. INCHOATE OFFENCES 101
    15.1 Attempt 101
        15.1.1 Proximity 101
        15.1.2 Impossibility 102
        15.1.3 Punishment on conviction 103
    15.2 Conspiracy 103
        15.2.1 Impossibility 104
        15.2.2 Punishment on conviction 104
    15.3 Incitement 104
        15.3.1 Impossibility 105
        15.3.2 Punishment on conviction 105
    15.4 Statute 106

16. INTRODUCTION TO DEFENCES 107

17. PROVOCATION AND EXCESSIVE SELF-DEFENCE 108
    17.1 Provocation at common law 108
        17.1.1 Which Characteristics are Relevant? 109
    17.2 Provocation in Irish Law 109

17.2.1 *People (DPP) v MacEoin [1978] I.R. 27* 110
17.2.2 What is provocation post-MacEoin? 110
17.2.3 Must the provocation be immediate? 110
17.2.4 Cumulative Provocation 111
17.2.5 What Amounts to Provocative Conduct? 111
17.2.6 Who must provoke? 112
17.2.7 Proportionality 112
17.3 Excessive Self-defence 112
17.3.1 What amounts to excessive self-defence? 112

18. INTOXICATION 114
18.1 Distinction between crimes of basic/specific intent ... 114
18.2 Voluntary/Involuntary Intoxication 115
18.3 Dutch Courage 116
18.4 Intoxication in Irish law 116

19. AUTOMATISM 118
19.1 Definition 118
19.2 Internal and External Factors 118
19.3 Self-Induced Automatism 119

20. INSANITY 122
20.1 The Criminal Law (Insanity) Act 2006 122
20.1.1 Section 4 Fitness to be tried 122
20.1.2 Section 5 Verdict 123
20.1.3 Section 6(1) Diminished Responsibility 124
20.1.4 Appeals 124
20.2 The Mental Health (Criminal Law) Review Board ... 124
20.3 The defence of Insanity 125
20.4 The M'Naghten Rules 125
20.4.1 Defect of Reason from a Disease
       of the Mind 126
20.4.2 Nature and Quality of the Act 127
20.4.3 The Wrongful Nature of the Act 127
20.4.4 Irresistible Impulse 128
20.4.5 The consequences of the plea of insanity 129

21. SELF-DEFENCE 130
21.1 Justifiable Use of Force 130
21.2 Force 132

22.	Infancy	133
	22.1 Children under the age of seven years	133
	22.2 Children between seven and 14 years	133
	22.3 The Children Act 2001	134
23.	Duress and Necessity	135
	23.1 Necessity	136
24.	Mistake	137
25.	Consent	138
26.	Preparing for a Criminal Law Exam	139
	26.1 Before the Exam	139
	26.2 The Exam	140
	26.3 Essay Questions	141
	26.4 Problem Questions	142
	26.5 After the Exam	142

Index 143

TABLE OF LEGISLATION

IRISH STATUTES

Air Pollution Act 1997
   s.11 45
Bail Act 1997 21
   s.1 21
   s.1(2) 21
   s.2 .... 21, 23
   s.2(1) 21
   s.2(2) 21
   s.3 21
   s.4 21
   s.5 21
   s.6 21
   s.10 .... 22, 24
Children Act 2001 134
   s.52 134
   s.52(2) 134
Criminal Assets Bureau Act
   1996 25
Criminal Damage Act
   1991 .... 68, 75
   s.1 75
   s.2 .... 68, 75, 77, 78
   s.2(1) 75, 76, 77
   s.2(2) 76, 77
   s.2(3) 76, 77
   s.3 77
   s.4 78
   s.5 .... 78, 81
   s.6 75
   s.7(2) 76
   s.14(1) 68, 77
Criminal Justice Act 1951
   Schedule 9
Criminal Justice Act 1957
   s.15(3) 15
Criminal Justice Act 1964
   s.4 47
   s.4(1) 46, 47

   s.4(2) 32, 47
Criminal Justice Act 1984 ... 22, 23
   s.4 15
   s.11 .... 20, 22, 24
Criminal Justice Act 1990 94
   s.1 49
   s.2 94
   s.3 .... 24, 48
   s.4 .... 49, 94
Criminal Justice Act 1991
   s.6(2)(c) 136
Criminal Justice Act 1993 26
Criminal Justice Act 1999 26
   s.38 47
Criminal Justice (Community
   Service) Act 1983 25
Criminal Justice
   (Public Order)
   Act 1994 .... 86, 92
   s.4 .... 86, 89
   s.4(3) 86, 87
   s.5 .... 86, 87, 89
   s.6 .... 86, 87, 89
   s.7 .... 88, 89
   s.7(1) 88
   s.8 89
   s.9 .... 88, 89
   s.14 89
   s.14(2) 89
   s.15 90
   s.15(1) 90
   s.15(3) 90
   s.15(5) 90
   s.15(6) 90
   s.16 91
   s.16(1) 91
   s.16(3) 91
   s.18 .... 91, 92
   s.19 92
   s.19(1) 92

s.19(1)(a) 92, 93
s.19(1)(b) 93
s.19(1)(c) 93
s.19(3) 93
Criminal Justice (Theft and Fraud
 Offences) Act 2001 . . 75, 78, 91
s.2(1) 79, 80
s.4 .... 79, 137
s.4(2) 79
s.4(4) 79, 80
s.5 80
s.5(2) 80
s.6 80
s.7 80
s.8 .... 80, 81
s.9 81
s.10 81
s.12 .... 81, 82
s.12(2) 82
s.12(4) 81
s.13 82
s.13(1) 82
s.13(2) 82
s.14 83
s.16(2) 84
s.17 84
s.18 84
s.18(2) 84
Criminal Justice (United Nations
 Conventions Against
 Torture) Act 2000 11
Criminal Law Act 1997 39
s.3 3
s.7 39
s.7(1) 39, 105
s.7(2) 42
s.8 39
Criminal Law (Amendment) Act
 1885 62
s.11 62
Criminal Law (Amendment) Act
 1935
s.1 44
s.1(1) 6, 7, 45, 53, 59, 60
s.1(2) 60

s.2 .... 59, 60
Criminal Law (Insanity) Act
 2006 . . 51, 118, 122, 125, 129
s.1 122
s.4 122
s.4(2) 122
s.5 .... 123, 128
s.6 51
s.6(1) 124
s.6(3) 51, 124
s.7 124
s.8 124
s.11 124
s.12 124
s.13 129
Criminal Law (Rape) Act 1981
s.2 57
s.2(1) 54
s.2(2) 56
Criminal Law (Rape)
 (Amendment) Act
 1990 .... 53, 54, 133
s.2 .... 57, 58
s.3 58
s.4 57
s.5 54
s.6 .... 54, 133
s.9 55
Criminal Law (Sexual Offences)
 Act 1993
s.2 138
s.3 .... 53, 61
s.4 62
s.5 60
Criminal Law (Sexual Offences)
 Act 2006 .... 53, 60, 61
s.2 .... 60, 61, 62
s.3 .... 60, 61, 62
Criminal Law (Suicide) Act 1993
s.2(1) 47
s.2(2) 47, 51
Criminal Lunatics Act 1800 ... 122
Criminal Procedure Act 1967
s.22 17
s.31 17

Table of Legislation

Drug Trafficking Act 1996
   s.2 15
Environmental Protection Agency
   Act 1992
   s.8 45
European Convention on
   Human Rights
   Act 2003 8
   s.2(1) 8
Forgery Act 1861 78
Forgery Act 1913 78
Geneva Conventions Act 1962 . . . 11
Genocide Act 1973 11
Infanticide Act 1949 51
   s.1 51
Larceny Act 1861 78
Larceny Act 1916 . . . . 78, 79
Larceny Act 1990 78
Mental Health Act 2001 129
Misuse of Drugs Act 1977
   s.15 24
Non Fatal Offences
   against the Person
   Act 1997 . . . . 64, 91, 141
   s.1 68
   s.2 . . . . 57, 64, 65, 66, 92
   s.2(1) 57, 64, 65
   s.2(1)(a) 64, 65
   s.2(1)(b) 64
   s.2(2) 65
   s.3 . . . . 65, 66
   s.4 . . . . 58, 66, 67
   s.5 67
   s.6 . . . . 46, 68
   s.6(1) 68
   s.6(2) 69, 70
   s.6(3) 69
   s.6(5) 69, 70
   s.6(5)(a) 69
   s.6(5)(b) 69
   s.6(5)(?) 70
   s.7 . . . . 68, 70
   s.8 . . . . 68, 70
   s.8(2) 71
   s.9 71
   s.10 71

   s.10(3) 72
   s.10(5) 72
   s.11 72
   s.13 73
   s.14 73
   s.15 73
   s.15(1) 73
   s.15(2) 73
   s.16 74
   s.17 74
   s.18 . . . . 130, 131, 132
   s.18(1) 131
   s.18(3)(b) 136
   s.18(5) 131
   s.18(7) 131
   s.19 . . . . 130, 132
   s.19(1) 132
   s.19(3) 132
   s.20 132
   s.20(3) 132
   s.20(4) 132
   s.21 . . . . 75, 136
   s.22(1) 130
   s.22(2) 130
Offences Against the Person Act
   1861 . . . . 32, 64, 102
   s.38 92
   s.61 . . . . 53, 61
   s.62 53
Offences Against the State Act
   1939 . . . . 5, 11, 48, 94, 96, 98
   s.10(1)(c) 95
   s.18 96
   s.19 . . . . 97, 100
   s.20 97
   s.21 99
   s.30 . . . . 15, 96, 98, 100
   s.52 98
   s.52(2) 98
   Schedule 11
Offences Against the State
   (Amendment) Act 1940 7
Offences Against the State
   (Amendment) Act 1972 . . . 98
   s.3 98
   s.3(2) 98, 99

Offences Against the State
   (Amendment) Act 1998 ... 99
   s.2 99
   s.6 99
   s.10 100
Official Secrets Act 1963 94
   s.4 95
   s.6 95
   s.9 95
   s.10 95
   s.13 96
Petty Sessions (Ireland)
   Act 1851 39
   s.22 105
Probation of Offenders
   Act 1907 26
   s.1(1) 26
   s.1(2) 26
Proceeds of Crime Act 1996 ... 25
   s.1(1) 25
Prohibition of Incitement
   to Hatred Act 1989 106
Prosecution of Offences
   Act 1974 5
Punishment of Incest Act
   1908 .... 42, 62
Sex Offenders Act 2001 63
Treason Act 1939 .... 11, 94
Trial of Lunatics Act 1883 ... 122
   s.2(2) 129

ENGLISH STATUTES

Accessories and Abettors
   Act 1861 39
   s.8 39
Homocide Act 1957
   s.3 109

OTHER TABLES

ARTICLES OF BUNREACHT NA HÉIREANN

Article 15 25
   15.2.1° 4
15.4.1° 4
15.5 4
15.13 4
26 .... 4, 7
30.1 4
30.3 4
34 .... 5, 7
34.3.1° 10
34.3.2° 5
35 5
37 5
38 .... 5, 25, 98
38.1 5
38.2 .... 5, 9
38.3 .... 6, 11
38.3.1° 5
38.4 6
38.5 5
38.5.2° 5
38.5.3° 5
38.5.4° 5
39 .... 11, 94
40 6
40.1 6
40.4 .... 6, 14
40.4.1° 17
40.4.2° 16
40.4.7° 20
40.6.1° 94
40.6.1°(i) 16
40.6.1°(ii) 6
50 .... 6, 109

ARTICLES OF THE EUROPEAN
CONVENTION ON HUMAN RIGHTS

Article 2 8
   3 8
   5 8
   6 .... 8, 33
   7 8
   8 8
   11 8

TABLE OF CASES

Irish cases

A v The Governor of Arbour Hill Prison [2006] I.E.S.C. 169 .... 16, 53
Article 26 and the Offences Against the State (Amendment)
    Act 1940, *In Re* [1940] I.R. 470 7
AG v Oldridge [2000] 4 I.R. 593 103
AG v Paperlink [1984] I.L.R.M. 373 15
C.C. v Ireland [2006] I.E.S.C. 33 .... 6, 45, 53, 59
Conroy v AG [1965] I.R. 411 9
Doyle v Wicklow County Council [1974] I.R. 55 .... 124, 125, 128
Ellis v DPP [1990] 2 I.R. 291 126
Gilligan v Criminal Assets Bureau [1998] 3 I.R. 185 25
Heaney v Ireland [1996] 1 I.R. 580 .... 16, 98
Hefferon Kearns Ltd, *In Re* [1993] 3 I.R. 191 34
Kennedy v Ireland [1987] I.R. 587 .... 6, 52
K.M. v DPP [1994] 1 I.R. 514 133
Melling v Ó Mathghamhna [1962] I.R. 1 9
Maguire v Shannon Regional Fisheries Board
    [1994] 2 I.L.R.M. 253 45
McGee v AG [1974] I.R. 587 52
O'Leary v Attorney General [1993] 1 I.R. 102 99
O'Laighleis, *In Re* [1960] I.R. 93 7
People v Healy [1989] 3 Frewen 188 22
People (AG) v Byrne [1974] I.R. 1 27
People (AG) v Capaldi [1949] 1 Frewen 95 104
People (AG) v Commane [1975] 1 Frewen 400 113
People (AG) v Crosbie [1966] I.R. 426 18
People (AG) v Crosbie & Meehan [1966] I.R. 490 49
People (AG) v Dermody [1956] I.R. 307 54
People (AG) v Dunleavy [1948] I.R. 95 .... 34, 50
People (AG) v Duffy [1942] I.R. 529 .... 18, 19
People (AG) v Dwyer [1972] I.R. 416 .... 113, 132
People (AG) v England [1947] 1 Frewen 81 101
People (AG) v Hayes, unreported, Court of Criminal Appeal,
    November 30, 1967 128
People (AG) v Keatley [1954] I.R. 12 .... 130, 131
People (AG) v Manning [1953] 89 I.L.T.R. 155 116
People (AG) v McGrath [1960] 1 Frewen 267 128
People (AG) v O'Callaghan [1966] I.R. 501 19
People (AG) v O'Brien [1936] I.R. 263 125

People (AG) v Ryan [1966] 1 Frewen 304 41
People (AG) v Sullivan [1964] I.R. 169 101
People (AG) v Thornton [1952] I.R. 91 101
People (AG) v Whelan [1934] I.R. 518 135
People (DPP) v Bambrick [1999] 2 I.L.R.M. 71 112
People (DPP) v Bartley, unreported, High Court, June 13, 1997 29
People (DPP) v Cagney, unreported, Court of Criminal
    Appeal, May 27, 2004 73
People (DPP) v Creighton [1994] 1 I.L.R.M. 551 56
People (DPP) v Cullagh, unreported, Court of Criminal
    Appeal, March 15, 1999 50
People (DPP) v Dennigan [1980] 3 Frewen 253 23
People (DPP) v Doolan [2002] 4 I.R. 463 43
People (DPP) v Douglas and Hayes [1985] I.L.R.M. 25 .... 32, 102
People (DPP) v Eccles, unreported, Court of Criminal
    Appeal, February 10, 1986 43
People (DPP) v Egan [1989] I.R. 681 42
People (DPP) v Farrell [1978] I.R. 336 16
People (DPP) v Ferguson, unreported, Court of Criminal
    Appeal, October 27, 1975 99
People (DPP) v Gallagher [1991] I.L.R.M. 339 .... 123, 129
People (DPP) v Healy [1990] I.L.R.M. 313 .... 16, 137
People (DPP) v Heaney, unreported, Court of Criminal
    Appeal, January 17, 2000 112
People (DPP) v Hendley, unreported, Court of Criminal
    Appeal, June 11, 1993 50
People (DPP) v Hull, unreported, Court of Criminal Appeal,
    July 8, 1996 32
People (DPP) v Kelly [2000] 2 I.R. 1 112
People (DPP) v Kehoe [1992] I.L.R.M. 481 111
People (DPP) v MacEoin [1978] I.R. 27 .... 109, 110, 111, 112
People (DPP) v Madden [1977] I.R. 336 42
People (DPP) v McBride [1997] I.L.R.M. 233 .... 32, 117
People (DPP) v McCreesh [1992] I.L.R.M. 239 14
People (DPP) v McDonagh [1996] 1 I.R. 565 56
People (DPP) v McGinley [1998] 2 I.L.R.M. 233 23
People (DPP) v McGrath, unreported, Court of Criminal
    Appeal, May 27, 2004 73
People (DPP) v Mullane, unreported, Court of Criminal
    Appeal, March 11, 1997 112
People (DPP) v Mulligan, unreported, Court of Criminal
    Appeal, May 17, 2004 99
People (DPP) v Murray [1977] I.R. 360 .... 13, 34, 43, 92, 93
People (DPP) v Noonan [1998] 2 I.R. 439; [1998] I.L.R.M. 154 .. 109, 112

Table of Cases xxiii

People (DPP) v O'Reilly [1991] 1 I.R. 77 40
People (DPP) v Pringle [1981] 2 Frewen 57 .... 16, 43
People (DPP) v Pringle [1997] 2 I.R. 225 .... 12, 13
People (DPP) v Quilligan [1986] I.R. 495 .... 11, 15, 96
People (DPP) v Ramachandran [2000] 2 I.R. 307 72
People (DPP) v Reid & Kirwan [2004] 1 I.R. 392 91
People (DPP) v Reilly [2004] I.E.C.C.A. 10 .... 117, 119
People (DPP) v Rose, unreported, Court of Criminal
    Appeal, February 21, 2002 41
People (DPP) v Shaw [1982] I.R. 1 6
People (DPP) v Shortt (No.2) [2002] 2 I.R. 696 12
People (DPP) v Wall, unreported, Court of Criminal
    Appeal, December 16, 2005 12
People (DPP) v Walsh [1980] I.R. 294 .... 14, 16
People (DPP) v X, unreported, Court of Criminal
    Appeal, 1995 55
PSS v JAS, unreported, High Court, May 22, 1995 34
Ryan v AG [1965] I.R. 294 .... 6, 52
Ryan v DPP [1989] I.R. 399 20
Savage v DPP [1982] I.L.R.M. 385 11
Shannon Regional Fisheries Board v Cavan County
    Council [1996] 3 I.R. 267 45
State v Purcell [1942] I.R. 207 .... 18, 19
State (Coughlan) v Minister for Justice [1968] I.L.T.R. 177 123
State (Healy) v Donoghue [1976] I.R. 325 .... 6, 16
State (Trombole) v Governor of Mountjoy Prison
    [1985] I.R. 306 14
Ward of Court (Withdrawal of Medical Treatment),
    In Re [1996] 2 I.R. 79 52

ENGLISH CASES

Alphacell Ltd v Woodward [1972] A.C. 824 45
Attorney General for Northern Ireland v Gallagher [1961]
    3 All E. R. 299 299
Attorney General's Reference (No. 1) [1975] 2 All E.R. 684 41
Bedder v DPP [1954] 2 All E.R. 801 .... 108, 109
Bratty v Attorney General for Northern Ireland [1963]
    3 All E.R. 523 118
Chang Wing-Siu v R [1985] A.C. 168 43
DPP v Beard [1920] All E.R. 21 114
DPP v Majewski [1976] 2 All E.R. 142 ..... 114, 115, 116, 117, 119, 120
DPP v Morgan [1975] 2 All E.R. 347 .... 56, 137
DPP v Nock [1978] A.C. 979 104

DPP v Stonehouse [1977] 2 All E.R. 909 102
Elliot v C (a minor) [1983] 2 All E.R. 1005 33
Fagan v Metropolitan Police Commissioner
  [1968] 3 All E.R. 442 35
Gillick v West Norfolk and Wisbeck Area Health Authority
  [1985] 3 All E.R 402 40
Hardcastle v Bielty [1982] 1 Q.B. 709 44
Houghton v Smith [1975] A.C. 476 101
Hyam v DPP [1974] 2 All E.R. 41 .... 31, 32
Kaitamaki v R. [1985] 2 All E.R. 435 .... 35, 54
Metropolitan Police Commissioner v Caldwell
  [1981] 1 All E.R. 901 33
Miller v Minister for Pensions [1947] All E.R. 372 28
R v Adomako [1994] 3 All E.R. 79 50
R v Ahluwalia [1993] 4 All E.R. 88 111
R v Allen [1988] Crim L.R. 698 116
R v Anderson & Morris [1966] 2 All E.R. 644 .... 42, 44
R v Bailey [1983] 2 All E.R. 503 .... 120, 121
R v Blaue [1975] 3 All E.R. 446 38
R v Boshears, The Times, February 8, 1961 118
R v Brown [1985] Crim. L.R. 212 82
R v Brown [1993] 2 All E.R. 75 .... 59, 67
R v Bubb (1851) 4 Cox C.C. 455 30
R v Calhaem [1985] 2 All E.R. 266 40
R v Camplin (1845) 1 Cox C.C. 220 55
R v Camplin [1978] 2 ALL E.R. 168 .... 108, 109
R v Cato [1976] 1 All E.R. 260 37
R v Cheshire [1991] 3 All E.R. 670 38
R v Church [1965] 2 All E.R. 72 36
R v Clarke [1972] 1 All E.R. 219 126
R v Clarkson [1971] 3 All E.R. 344 41
R v Clegg [1995] 1 All E.R. 334 113
R v Codere (1916) 12 Cr. App. Rep. 21 127
R v Court [1988] 2 All E.R. 221 57
R v Creighton (1909) 14 Cox C.C. 349 128
R v Cunningham [1957] 2 All E.R. 412 33
R v Deller (1952) 36 Cr. App. Rep. 184 28
R v Dickie [1984] 3 All E.R. 173 127
R v Doughty [1986] Crim L.R. 625 111
R v Dudley & Stephens (1884) Cox C.C. 624 136
R v Duffy [1949] 1 All E.R. 932 108
R v Dytham [1979] 3 All E.R 641 .... 29, 41
R v Eagleton (1855) 169 E.R. 66 101
R v Fitzmaurice [1983] 1 All E.R. 189 104

Table of Cases

R v Flattery (1877) 13 Cox C.C. 388 ... 55
R v G & R [2003] 4 All E.R. 765 ... 34
R v Gianetto [1996] Crim. L.R. 722 ... 40, 41
R v Gibbins & Proctor (1918) 13 Cr. App. Rep. 134 ... 30
R v Gorrie [1919] 83 J.P. 136 ... 133
R v Hadfield (1800) 27 St Tr 1281 ... 125
R v Hancock and Shankland [1986] 1 All E.R. 641 ... 31
R v Hardie [1984] 3 All E.R. 848 ... 115
R v Instan (1893) 17 Cox C.C. 602 ... 50
R v Ireland [1997] 4 All E.R. 225 ... 65
R v Jordan (1956) 40 Cr. App. Rep. 152 ... 37
R v Kemp [1957] 1 Q.B. 399 ... 126
R v Kingston [1994] 3 All E.R. 353 ... 116
R v Kimber [1983] 3 All E.R. 316 ... 137
R v Kopsch (1925) 19 Cr. App. Rep. 50 ... 128
R v Lang (1972) 62 Cr. App. Rep. 50 ... 55
R v Larsonneur (1933) 29 Cox C.C. 673 ... 28
R v Latimer (1886) 16 Cox C.C. 70 ... 46
R v Lawrence [1981] 1 All E.R. 974 ... 33
R v Linekar [1995] 3 All E.R. 69 ... 55
R v Lipman [1970] 1 Q.B. 152 ... 115
R v Maloney [1985] 1 All E.R. 1025 ... 31
R v Mayers (1872) 12 Cox C.C. 311 ... 55
R v McInnes [1973] 3 All E.R. 295 ... 132
R v Miller [1983] 1 All E.R. 978 ... 29, 36
R v M'Naghten [1843] All E.R. 229 ... 125
R v Nedrick [1986] 3 All E.R. 1 ... 32
R v Newell (1980) 71 Cr. App. Rep 331 ... 109
R v Olugboja [1981] 3 All E.R. 443 ... 55
R v Paggett [1983] Crim.L.R. 394 ... 37
R v Pommell [1995] 2 Cr. App. Rep. 607 ... 136
R v Quick [1973] 3 All E.R. 347 ... 120, 126
R v Satnam and Kewal [1988] Crim. L.R. 236 ... 56
R v Senior (1899) 19 Cox C.C. 219 ... 51
R v Shepard (1987) 86 Cr. App. Rep. 47 ... 135
R v Smith [1959] 2 All E.R. 193 ... 38
R v Stone & Dobinson [1977] 2 All E.R. 341 ... 29, 51
R v Sullivan [1983] 2 All E.R. 673 ... 126
R v T [1990] Crim L.R. 607 ... 119
R v Thornton (No.2) [1996] 2 All E.R. 1023 ... 111
R v Tolson (1889) 23 Q.B.D. 706 ... 137
R v White [1910] All E.R. 340 ... 36
R v Whitehouse [1977] 3 All E.R. 737 ... 105
R v Williams [1922] All E.R. 433 ... 55

R v Windle [1952] 2 All E.R. 1 .... 125, 127
R v Woolin [1999] 1 A.C. 82 32
Race Relations Board v Applin [1974] 2 W.L.R. 541 104
Tesco Supermarkets Ltd v Natrass [1972] A.C. 153 45
Thabo Meli v R [1954] 1 All E.R. 37 36
Tubberville v Savage (1661) 1 Mod Rep. 3 65
Winzar v Chief Constable of Kent, The Times, March 28, 1983 29
Woolmington v DPP [1935] All E.R. 1 .... 27, 107

AUSTRALIAN CASES

R v Jenson and Ward [1980] VR 1904 44
R v O'Connor (1980) 146 C.L.R. 64 .... 115, 117
R v Orton [1922] V.L.R. 469 103
R v Taktak (1988) 34 A. Crim. R. 334 .... 30, 51

CANADIAN CASES

Canadian Dredge and Dock Co. v R [1985] I.S.C.R. 662 45
Leary v R (1977) 74 D.L.R. (3d) 103 117
R v Bernard [1988] 2 S.C.R. 833 117
R v Daviault [1994] 3 S.C.R. 63 .... 115, 117

NORTHERN IRISH CASES

Devlin v Armstrong [1971] N.I. 13 131
R v Fitzpatrick [1997] N.I. 20 135
R v Porter [1980] N.I. 18 103

ECHR CASES

Laskey, Jaggard & Brown v UK [1997] E.H.R.R. 59 59
Norris v Ireland (1991) 13 E.H.R.R. 186 61

1. INTRODUCTION

It is impossible in a book of this nature to cover in any great depth all aspects of an area of law as broad and diverse as the criminal law. Its objective then, is to set out the most fundamental principles of law as they operate in this jurisdiction. Before looking at the substantive areas covered by the criminal law, which are contained in subsequent chapters, a few general points need to be made about this area of the law and its function in this, or indeed any society.

1.1 THE FUNCTION OF THE CRIMINAL LAW

The behaviour of individuals in any society is subject to regulation in a number of ways. Social norms and customs, religion and the laws of any jurisdiction are just some of the methods through which the behaviour of human beings can be curtailed in an attempt to establish and maintain a peaceful and ordered society. Of all these methods, the criminal law is unique in that it is the only method of social control which is enforced by means of state-imposed sanctions on the transgressing individual. The criminal law of any jurisdiction sets out the various types of behaviour which are deemed to be unacceptable to the members of that society and which are considered to be sufficiently serious to warrant the involvement of the state. Unlike other areas of law such as the law of contract and the law of tort, both of which involve disputes between private individuals, the criminal law is an area of public law in which the individual against whom allegations of criminal activity are made is prosecuted by the state in the name of the people and, if convicted, will be subject to court-imposed sanctions which are prescribed by law and enforced by the Executive.

In this jurisdiction, criminal activity is that which is expressly prohibited by statute. In addition, there are numerous offences recognised by the common law and a very small number which are provided for by Bunreacht na hÉireann. Regardless of the source of the offence, all remain subject to the requirements of Bunreacht na hÉireann. Society's interest in the suppression of criminal activity and the effective operation of its criminal justice system requires a coherent body of rules, an impartial and independent judiciary and an adequately resourced and trained police force. On the other hand, the seriousness of the consequences to the individual charged with a criminal offence requires that at all stages, from the investigation of an offence through to the outcome of a criminal trial, the individual is possessed of numerous rights provided for by law. Anyone charged with a criminal offence in this jurisdiction is entitled by law to be presumed innocent until the contrary be proven beyond a reasonable doubt before an impartial judge and, subject to certain exceptions, a jury. While it will normally be in society's interests to prosecute criminal activity, there are instances in which this interest must yield to a greater interest in protecting the individual. For this reason, certain categories of people are deemed to be incapable of committing a criminal offence. The doctrine of *doli incapax* creates an irrebuttable presumption of incapacity in the case of children under the age of seven. This presumption also applies to children between the ages of seven and 14 years of age, but in these cases the presumption is rebuttable and children in this age group may be deemed to be *doli capax* and therefore liable to stand trial where it can be shown that the child could distinguish between right and wrong.

In addition, there are various defences available to the individual charged with a criminal offence. These can operate in such a way as to either excuse or justify the behaviour of the defendant. The right of an accused person to be presumed innocent places the burden of proof on the prosecution, who must not only prove all the elements of the charge(s) against the accused, beyond a reasonable doubt, but also negative any defence(s) and/or explanations put forward by the defence which are consistent with the innocence of the accused.

2. SOURCES OF CRIMINAL LAW

The primary sources of Irish criminal law are legislation and the common law, both of which will be discussed briefly. The role played by Bunreacht na hÉireann is of fundamental importance, since it provides the framework within which the criminal law must operate.

Like other areas of law, the criminal law may be said to come from different sources. These are mainly legislation/statute and the common law.

2.1 STATUTE

As provided for by Bunreacht na hÉireann, sole legislative power is vested in the Oireachtas, with the caveat that any legislation enacted must comply with constitutional requirements such as the prohibition on the enactment of legislation which is retrospective in effect and that which is unconstitutional by virtue of its incompatibility with any of the provisions of Bunreacht na hÉireann. Criminal statutes may be enacted to create entirely new offences, to codify existing common law rules or to add to existing common law offences.

2.2 COMMON LAW

Since the enactment of Bunreacht na hÉireann with its prohibition on law-making by any body other than the Oireachtas, judges have not been able to declare acts to be illegal as they had been able to for centuries. Nevertheless, the common law remains a very important legal resource in that many of the rules and principles which are employed by the courts have been created by the common law courts. The decisions of courts in other common law jurisdictions, which, although not binding on Irish courts, are of persuasive value. At common law, offences were categorised as treasons, felonies and misdemeanours, the first two types being the most serious and the latter being less grave in nature. The distinction between felonies and misdemeanours was abolished in this jurisdiction by s.3 of the Criminal Law Act 1997, which replaced the category of felonies with a new classification of offences, known as arrestable offences. An arrestable offence is defined as one which carries a potential sentence of five years or more. Offences are also categorised as "indictable" or "summary". Indictable offences are tried on indictment in the Circuit,

Central or Special Criminal Courts or in some cases in the District Court if the offence in question is an "either-or" offence, subject to the conditions outlined in the paragraph relating to the criminal jurisdiction of the District Court. Summary offences are less serious in nature and are dealt with in the District Court.

2.3 The impact of Bunreacht na hÉireann 1937

Bunreacht na hÉireann 1937 is the primary source of law in this jurisdiction. A number of articles in Bunreacht na hÉireann are of particular relevance to the criminal law. The following is a brief outline of those:

Article 15.2.1 vests sole law-making power in the Oireachtas. Due to the operation of the doctrine of the Separation of Powers, no other body, including the judicial arm of the State, has the power to make law.

Article 15.4.1 precludes the Oireachtas from enacting any law that is repugnant to any part of Bunreacht na hÉireann.

Article 15.5 forbids the enactment of any legislation that is retrospective in its effect. This is in keeping with the maxim *nullem crimen sine lege, nulla poena sine lege* which translates as "no crime without law, no punishment without law".

Article 15.13 provides immunity from arrest for criminal offences (except treason) for any member of either House of Oireachtas, going to, coming from or while within the precincts of either House of the Oireachtas.

Article 26 provides for the procedure by which the President may, after consultation with the Council of State, refer a Bill to the Supreme Court for a determination as to its constitutionality. If a Bill survives a challenge under the Article, it must be signed into law by the President and is immune from further challenge.

Article 30.1 provides for the office of the Attorney General who is the legal advisor to the Government.

Article 30.3 provides that all crimes other than summary offences shall be prosecuted in the name of the People and at the suit of the Attorney General "or some other person authorised in accordance with law to act for that purpose". Since the establishment of the Office of the Director of Public Prosecutions pursuant to the provisions of the Prosecution of Offences Act 1974, the vast majority of prosecutions are taken by the DPP although there appears to be nothing to stop the Attorney General from prosecuting any non-summary offence, and there are a small number of offences that may only be prosecuted by the Attorney General.

Article 34 and its subsections relate to the courts. Provision is made for the establishment of Courts of First Instance and a Court of Final Appeal. Under Art.34, the High Court is vested with "full original jurisdiction in and power to determine all matters and questions whether of law or fact, civil or criminal".

Article 34.3.2 is of particular importance in that it provides that only the High Court has jurisdiction to determine the constitutionality of any law, subject to an appeal to the Supreme Court.

Article 35 relates to the appointment and tenure of judges.

Article 37 provides that limited powers of a judicial nature may be exercised by a person or body of persons other than a judge or a court. Criminal matters are expressly excluded from this, which means that no person or body of persons, other than a judge or a court, can determine matters of a criminal nature.

Article 38 deals with the Trial of Offences and provides in subs.(1) that "no person shall be tried on any criminal charge save in due course of law".

Article 38.2 states that minor offences may be tried by courts of summary jurisdiction.

Article 38.3.1 declares that "special courts may be established by law for the trial of offences in cases where it may be determined in accordance with such law that the ordinary courts are inadequate to secure the effective administration of justice, and the preservation of public peace and order". The Special Criminal Court was set up under the Offences Against the State Act 1939—pursuant to the terms of this article and its subsections.

Article 38.5 provides that "save in the case of the trial of offences under Section 2, Section 3 or Section 4 of this Article, no person shall be tried on any criminal charge without a jury". This means that summary trials (Art.38.2), trials in the Special Criminal Court

(Art.38.3) and trials before Military Tribunals (Art.38.4) are not required to take place before a jury and that the trial of an accused person in these circumstances is not unconstitutional by virtue of the absence of a jury.

Article 40 deals with fundamental rights. Many of these are enumerated, such as Personal Liberty (Art.40.1) and Freedom of Assembly (Art.40.6.1(ii)). Others are unenumerated but are no less significant. Examples of unenumerated personal rights include:

> Privacy—held in *Kennedy v Ireland* [1987] I.R. 587.
> Bodily Integrity—held in *Ryan v AG* [1965] I.R. 294.
> Free legal aid in criminal cases—held in *State (Healy) v Donoghue* [1976] I.R. 325.

Article 40.4 provides for the procedure known as *habeas corpus* whereby a person may question the legality of his detention.

Article 50 provides that laws in force in Saorstát Éireann immediately prior to the enactment of Bunreacht na hÉireann will be deemed to have been "carried over" into the law of the new State, provided that they are not inconsistent with the provisions of Bunreacht na hÉireann and that they have not been repealed. Any statutory provision or rule of common law that preceded the enactment of Bunreacht na hÉireann is challenged under Art.50, the most recent example of which was the challenge to s.1(1) of the Criminal Law Amendment Act 1935 which was deemed to be unconstitutional in *CC v Ireland and the Attorney General* [2006] I.E.S.C. 33.

In the context of the criminal law, two important factors should be noted.

> (1) Breaches of the constitutional rights of an accused person may well lead to an arrest, detention, prosecution or trial being invalid. It must be said however, that no right is absolute and even a constitutionally protected right may have to give way to a superior right or interest on occasion. *People (DPP) v Shaw* [1982] I.R. 1, is one such example. In this case, a confession obtained at a time when the accused was being detained unconstitutionally was nevertheless admitted into evidence on the basis that the Gardaí had

breached his constitutional right to liberty in order to vindicate the right to life of a woman who had been kidnapped by the accused. Unknown to Gardaí, the woman had, in fact, been murdered by the accused. In this case, it was held that the woman's right to life took precedence over the accused's right to liberty and the evidence was allowed.

(2) Legislation or rules of common law can be challenged using the process known as judicial review. The net effect of a finding of unconstitutionality is that the legislation or common law rule in question is of no legal consequence. Different considerations apply depending on the vintage of the impugned law. If the legislation or rule of common law predates the enactment of Bunreacht na hÉireann, the question for the court will be whether it was "carried over" into the law of the modern Irish State—such laws do not enjoy any presumption of constitutionality and if they are found to be repugnant to the terms of Bunreacht na hÉireann, are deemed not to have been carried over and never to have been valid in this jurisdiction. The most recent pre-1937 law to have been struck down in this fashion was s.1(1) of the Criminal Law (Amendment) Act 1935—which related to what is commonly known as "statutory rape". (See Chapter on Sexual Offences). Where the impugned law was passed after the enactment of the constitution, it is reviewed under Art.34. Any law passed since 1937 (including Bills) is presumed to be constitutional. Where such a law is then found to be unconstitutional it is declared to have been void *ab initio,* in other words, it was never valid. In the case of Bills, any Bill that survives a challenge under Art.26 is then immune from further challenge, even if constitutional rights are subsequently infringed by it. In *Re Ó Laighléis* [1960] I.R. 93, the plaintiff had been interned without trial pursuant to the provisions of the Offences Against the State (Amendment) Act 1940. He challenged the Act on the basis that it infringed his constitutional rights. However, the Act had been passed following an unsuccessful Art.26 challenge in *Re Article 26 and the Offences Against the State (Amendment) Bill 1940* [1940] I.R. 470, and was therefore immune from further challenge.

2.4 THE EUROPEAN CONVENTION ON HUMAN RIGHTS (ECHR)

Prior to the incorporation of the European Convention on Human Rights into domestic law by the European Convention on Human Rights Act 2003, Ireland did have international obligations under the Convention, and was amenable to the jurisdiction of the European Court of Human Rights. This however, did not mean that the Convention could be invoked before the Irish courts. Consequently, an individual who alleged that his rights under the Convention had been breached had to take his case to the European Court of Human Rights in Strasbourg in order to have the right in question vindicated.

2.5 THE EUROPEAN CONVENTION ON HUMAN RIGHTS ACT 2003

Having opted to incorporate the ECHR into domestic law at sub-constitutional level, the legislature has ensured that the status of the Constitution remains the same. However, s.2(1) of the Act provides that "in interpreting and applying any statutory provision or rule of law, a court shall, in so far as is possible, subject to the rules of law relating to such interpretation and application, do so in a manner compatible with the State's obligations under the Convention provisions". The Act requires that the courts interpret legislation "in so far as is possible" in conformity with the provisions of the Convention. This is likely to mean that the courts will continue to interpret legislation in conformity with the provisions of Bunreacht na hÉireann even where this might mean that to do so would not be in keeping with the terms of the ECHR. This will mean that applicants will still have to go to Strasbourg to let the European Court of Human Rights adjudicate on the matter. The only obligation imposed by the Act is that where a rule of law or statutory provision is declared by a court to be incompatible with the terms of the ECHR, the Taoiseach must cause a statement to be made in both Houses of the Oireachtas to that effect. The Oireachtas is not obliged to enact legislation that will accord with the provisions of the Convention, which could mean that legislation which is deemed to be incompatible with the Convention will remain on the books, although it will still be open to an aggrieved individual to pursue the matter before the European Court of Human Rights. In the context of criminal law, the most important rights covered by the Convention are: Life (Art.2); Freedom from Torture/inhuman/degrading treatment (Art.3); Liberty (Art.5); Fair trial (Art.6); Non-retrospectivity in criminal law legislation (Art.7); Expression (Art.8) and Freedom of peaceful assembly (Art.11).

3. THE JURISDICTION OF THE IRISH COURTS IN CRIMINAL MATTERS

3.1 THE DISTRICT COURT

The country is divided into 24 districts, the Dublin Metropolitan District and 23 others outside Dublin. The 23 Districts outside Dublin are sub-divided into 200 smaller districts, each with its own sitting of the District Court. Each District Court is a court of local and limited jurisdiction and in the context of criminal offences, is a court of summary jurisdiction. The court is presided over by a judge sitting without a jury. Article 38.2 of Bunreacht na hÉireann provides that minor offences may be tried summarily, although it is silent on the issue of what constitutes a minor offence.

In *Melling v Ó Mathghamhna* [1962] I.R. 1, the Supreme Court stated that when deciding whether an offence was minor, regard should be had to two factors:

(1) the severity of the punishment attracted by the offence; and
(2) the nature of the offence itself.

See also *Conroy v AG* [1965] I.R. 411.

Where an offence is provided for by statute, it will indicate whether an offence is one capable of being tried summarily.

The District Court is a court of limited and summary jurisdiction and may deal with:

(i) Cases in the district court area in which the alleged offence was committed.
(ii) Cases in the area where the defendant lives or carries out business.
(iii) Cases in the area in which the defendant was arrested.

As well as dealing with summary offences, the District Court can also deal with what are called "either way" offences. Certain offences, contained in the Schedule to the Criminal Justice Act 1951, may be tried on indictment or summarily in the District Court. These offences are subject to certain conditions being fulfilled.

(1) The District Court Judge must accept jurisdiction.
(2) The accused must consent to the offence being tried summarily—bearing in mind that he will forego his right to be tried by a jury.

(3) The consent of the DPP may also be required for the summary trial of the offence in question.

Indictable offences will also be sent forward by the District Court for trial upon service of the Book of Evidence.

3.2 THE CIRCUIT COURT

The country is divided into eight circuits, each Circuit Court being a court of local jurisdiction. The Circuit Court has jurisdiction to try all indictable offences with the exception of those which can only be tried before the Central Criminal Court. In addition to its first instance jurisdiction with regard to most indictable offences, the Circuit Court has appellate jurisdiction of decisions of the District Court. An appeal against conviction in the District Court may be made to the Circuit Court. The matter is then dealt with *de novo* by the Circuit Court and no appeal lies from that decision.

This court sits with a judge and jury and may deal with:

(i) Cases in the circuit court area in which the alleged offence was committed.
(ii) Cases in the area where the defendant lives or carries out business.
(iii) Cases in the area in which the defendant was arrested.

Cases may be transferred from one part of a circuit to another. Where the Director of Public Prosecutions or the accused applies for a transfer of a case, the circuit court judge may, if satisfied that it would be manifestly unfair not to do so, transfer a trial from the circuit court sitting outside Dublin to the Dublin Circuit Court.

The court has jurisdiction to try all non-minor offences except murder, rape, aggravated sexual assault, treason, piracy and related offences.

3.3 THE HIGH COURT/THE CENTRAL CRIMINAL COURT

Article 34.3.1 of Bunreacht na hÉireann provides that the High Court has "full jurisdiction in and power to determine all matters and questions whether of law or fact, civil or criminal".

The High Court, when exercising its criminal jurisdiction, is known as the Central Criminal Court. The court is presided over by a judge sitting with a jury. The court deals with those criminal offences which are outside the jurisdiction of the Circuit Court. These are:

- murder, attempted murder, conspiracy to murder;
- treason—defined in Art.39 of Bunreacht na hÉireann and provided for by the Treason Act 1939;
- piracy;
- certain offences under the Offences Against the State Act 1939;
- rape, aggravated sexual assault and attempted aggravated sexual assault;
- offences against the Genocide Act 1973;
- offences against the Geneva Conventions Act 1962;
- offences under the Criminal Justice (United Nations Conventions Against Torture) Act 2000.

The High Court has jurisdiction to deal with questions sent to it on a "case stated" basis. Where the District Court refers a matter to the High Court while a case is ongoing, the procedure is referred to as a "consultative case stated".

3.4 THE SPECIAL CRIMINAL COURT

This court was set up under Pt V of the Offences Against the State Act 1939 and is one of the constitutionally permissible instances in which an accused person may be tried without a jury. The constitutional basis for the court is to be found in Art.38.3 which provides that "Special Courts may be established by law for the trial of offences in cases where it may be determined in accordance with such law that the ordinary courts are inadequate to secure the effective administration of justice, and the preservation of public peace and order". The Special Criminal Court sits with three judges and no jury.

Offences contained in the Schedule to the Offences Against the State Act 1939 are dealt with by the court as are offences in respect of which the Director of Public Prosecutions has issued a certificate declaring that, in his opinion, the ordinary courts are inadequate to secure the administration of justice. In effect, therefore, any serious offence can come before the Special Criminal Court, even those which have no "subversive" element. See, for example, *People (DPP) v Quilligan* [1986] I.R. 495. In *Savage v DPP* [1982] I.L.R.M. 385, the court stated that the decisions of the Director of Public Prosecutions are generally not amenable to judicial review.

3.5 THE COURT OF CRIMINAL APPEAL

The Court of Criminal Appeal sits with three judges and has appellate jurisdiction only. The court can hear appeals against convictions from the Circuit, Central and Special Criminal Courts. Appeals are heard on the basis that the trial judge(s) have granted leave to appeal or where such leave to appeal has been refused, the Court of Criminal Appeal may itself grant leave to appeal. An appeal against conviction is premised on the assertion that the trial judge(s) either erred in law or that the trial was unsatisfactory for some other reason.

In cases involving appeals against conviction, the Court of Criminal Appeal can either:

(a) affirm the conviction.
(b) allow the appeal and order a re-trial.
(c) allow the appeal and enter an acquittal.

The Court of Criminal Appeal also hears appeals against sentence. These appeals can be made by either the convicted person on the basis that the sentence is too harsh or by the prosecution who may appeal against the leniency of the sentence. In either case, the court looks at whether the sentence imposed deviated from the range of sentences usually handed down for that particular offence with regard to the circumstances of the convicted person and of the offence itself.

Both these types of appeals are dealt with on the basis of the transcripts from the trial courts. In cases in which a miscarriage of justice is alleged due to the existence of a newly discovered fact, the court will hear this new evidence. If the court is satisfied that a miscarriage of justice has taken place, it may issue a certificate to that effect, which will then result in a payment of compensation for the aggrieved party. In *People (DPP) v Pringle* [1997] 2 I.R. 225, it was held that there was no exhaustive definition of "miscarriage of justice" and that furthermore, no such definition should be attempted. In *People (DPP) v Nora Wall* (Court of Criminal Appeal, December 16, 2005), the court gave some examples of situations which could amount to miscarriages of justice but said that the list was not definitive. These examples include: where the innocence of the accused is established; where the prosecution ought not to have been pursued due to a lack of credible evidence; where the trial was conducted in a manner inconsistent with judicial or constitutional procedure; and where, as occurred in *People (DPP) v Frank Shortt (No.2)* [2002] 2 I.R. 696, there had been a grave defect in the administration of justice brought on by the agents of the State.

3.6 THE SUPREME COURT

An appeal lies to the Supreme Court from a decision of the Court of Criminal Appeal where the latter court, the DPP or the AG certify that "a point of law of exceptional public importance" has arisen from the case in question which requires, in the public interest, a decision of the Supreme Court. See for example:

People (DPP) v Murray [1977] I.R. 360.
People (DPP) v Pringle [1997] 2 I.R. 225.

4. ARREST AND DETENTION

Article 40.4 of Bunreacht na hÉireann provides that "no citizen shall be deprived of his personal liberty save in accordance with law". Subsequent subsections of the Article lay out the procedure known as *habeas corpus* which is an investigation into the legality of detention. The *habeas corpus* procedure will be outlined later.

4.1 ARREST

An arrest, at common law, was defined by O'Higgins C.J. in *People (DPP) v Walsh* [1980] I.R. 294, as being:

> "the actual or notional seizure of a person for the purpose of imprisonment."

In *People (DPP) v McCreesh* [1992] I.L.R.M. 239, the Supreme Court defined an arrest in the following terms:

> "an arrest consists in or involves the seizure or touching of a person's body accompanied by a form of words which indicate to that person that he is under restraint. Whilst the older cases held that words alone would not suffice to constitute an arrest, nowadays words alone may amount to an arrest, if, in the circumstances they are calculated to bring, and do bring, to the person's notice that he is under restraint and he submitted to the compulsion." (*per* Hederman J.)

A person may generally only be arrested for the purpose of bringing him before a court to be charged with an offence. This may be done with or, in some cases, without a warrant. There must be a reasonable suspicion, backed up by evidence, that the suspect has committed an offence. In *State (Trimbole) v Governor of Mountjoy Prison* [1985] I.R. 306, an arrest was carried out in the absence of any reasonable cause to believe an offence had been committed. Gardaí arrested the individual for the sole purpose of detaining him pending the arrival of an extradition warrant. Due to the fact that there was no other reason to arrest him, his release was ordered on the grounds that his arrest was unlawful.

Once arrested, the suspect must be brought before the District Court to be charged with the offence, at the earliest practicable opportunity, even if this means that a special sitting of the District Court must be arranged. An exception to this occurs where the suspect is arrested after 10pm. In these situations, it is permissible to hold that person overnight until the court sits the following morning; this is provided for by s.15(3) of the Criminal Justice Act 1957.

There is no general right to arrest for questioning. However, there are some exceptions to this general rule and they are as follows:

(1) Under s.4 of the Criminal Justice Act 1984, a suspect may be detained for questioning for an initial period of six hours. This initial period may be extended by another six hours by a Garda of the rank of Superintendent or higher. The maximum permissible period of detention under s.4 is 12 hours.

(2) Under s.30 of the Offences Against the State Act 1939, a person arrested on suspicion of an offence "scheduled" to the Act may be detained for an initial period of 24 hours. A further period of 24 hours may be granted with the consent of a member of the Gardaí of the rank of Chief Superintendent or higher. Another period of 24 hours may be granted by a District Judge. The maximum permissible period of detention under s.30 is therefore 72 hours. The constitutionality of s.30 was upheld by the Supreme Court in *People (DPP) v Quilligan* [1987] I.L.R.M. 606.

(3) Section 2 of the Drug Trafficking Act 1996 allows for a suspect to be detained for an initial period of six hours. Further extensions may be granted as follows:

- A further period of 18 hours may be granted with the consent of a Chief Superintendent.
- Another 24 hour period may subsequently be granted, again with the consent of a Chief Superintendent.
- A further period of 72 hours may be granted where a District or Circuit Court Judge consents.
- Finally, another period of 48 hours may be granted with the consent of a District or Circuit Court Judge. The maximum period of detention under this Act is 168 hours/seven days.

4.2 RIGHTS ON ARREST AND DURING DETENTION

(1) A suspect has the right to remain silent and to be made aware of that right. This right is seen as a corollary of the right to communicate held in *AG v Paperlink [1984]*

I.L.R.M. 373, and that of Freedom of Expression as provided by Art.40.6.1(i) of Bunreacht na hÉireann and was the ruling of the Supreme Court in *Heaney v Ireland* [1994] 1 I.R. 580.
(2) A suspect must be told why he is being arrested—*People (DPP) v Walsh* [1980] I.R. 294. This does not necessarily mean that the precise provision of the Act in question must be cited to the suspect, but he must be given the reason for his arrest.
(3) A suspect has the right to legal aid if he cannot afford legal representation—*State (Healy) v Donoghue* [1976] I.R. 325.
(4) A suspect has the right to consult with a lawyer. Failure by the Gardaí to allow for this will render the suspect's detention unlawful—*People (DPP) v Healy* [1990] I.L.R.M. 313. A suspect has the right to privacy in his consultations with his lawyer but does not have the right to:
   (a) be informed of his right to see a lawyer—*People (DPP) v Farrell* [1978] I.R. 336.
   (b) have his lawyer present during interrogation—*People (DPP) v Pringle* [1981] 2 Frewen 57.
(5) A suspect has the right to food, rest and medical treatment.
(6) A suspect has the right of access to the courts.

4.3 HABEAS CORPUS

A person who wishes to question the validity of his detention may invoke the procedure known as *habeas corpus*. This procedure involves an inquiry under Art.40.4.2 of Bunreacht na hÉireann which is a two stage process.

The first step involves an application to the High Court or any judge thereof, by the person detained or by someone on his behalf, for a conditional order compelling the person causing the detention to provide the court with justification in writing for the detention. Under the terms of Bunreacht na hÉireann, the matter must be looked into "forthwith".

The second step involves the making of an absolute order directing the release of the prisoner if his detention is not in accordance with law. The person causing the detention must be given the opportunity to be heard on the matter and an appeal lies to the Supreme Court for the decision of the High Court. See, for example, *A v The Governor of Arbour Hill Prison* [2006] I.E.S.C. 169.

5. BAIL

Article 40.4.1 of Bunreacht na hÉireann states that "no citizen shall be deprived of his personal liberty save in due course of law". The issue of bail arises in two situations. The first of these is where an accused person has been charged with an offence and wishes to be released on bail pending the date of his trial. The second of these situations occurs where the accused, having been convicted, wishes to appeal against either his conviction or the sentence imposed by the court and applies to be released on bail until the hearing of his appeal. For the purposes of this chapter, the issue of bail will be dealt with in the context of the former of the two situations, this being the more usual of the two.

Essentially, bail is a form of conditional release, the main condition being that the accused person will turn up to face trial. Bail is granted upon the accused person entering into a recognisance, with or without sureties. What this means is that the accused person agrees to abide by whatever conditions the court may impose, and crucially, that he will show up to face trial. Breach of any bail conditions or failure to attend for his trial by the accused will lead to the issuing of a bench warrant for his arrest and the forfeiture of whatever sum of money has been lodged either by the accused person himself or by a third party on his behalf. He may also be arrested without warrant. The main issue that arises in the context of bail is that of the valid grounds upon which bail may be refused. It must be borne in mind that at this stage, the accused person has not yet been tried for the offence in question, much less convicted of it.

5.1 JURISDICTION TO GRANT BAIL

Jurisdiction to grant bail was provided for by s.31 of the Criminal Procedure Act 1967—which allowed for what was known as "station bail". The Sergeant/Member in Charge of a Garda station could "if he considers it prudent to do so and no warrant directing the detention of that person is in force, release him on bail and for that purpose take from him a recognisance, with or without sureties, for his due appearance before the District Court at the appropriate time and place."

Jurisdiction was also vested in the District Court by s.22 of the same Act—this section provided that where the District Court remands a person or sends him forward for trial or sentence, the court may either: (a) commit him to prison or other lawful custody; or (b) release him conditionally on his entering a recognisance, with or without sureties. The decision of the District Court may be appealed to the High Court, which also has jurisdiction to grant bail at first instance.

Admission to bail usually involves the accused and his sureties acknowledging that they are liable to forfeit a sum of money if bail conditions are disobeyed.

5.2 VALID GROUNDS FOR REFUSAL OF BAIL

The traditional view had been that if there was a possibility that the accused would commit another offence while on bail, the court would be entitled to take this into account when deciding whether to grant bail. The criteria governing the granting or refusal of bail were laid down by Hanna J. in *State v Purcell* [1942] I.R. 207. These were:

(a) The seriousness of the charge faced by the accused.
(b) The severity of the punishment imposed by law.
(c) The strength of the case against the accused.
(d) The prospect of a reasonably speedy trial.
(e) The opposition of the Attorney General.

In *AG v Duffy* [1942] I.R. 529, Hanna J. added another criterion to the list, which was that if there was evidence that the accused was likely to interfere with the course of justice, the court would be entitled to consider this as a material ground against bail being granted.

The Supreme Court endorsed the criteria set down by Hanna J. in *Purcell* and *Duffy* in *People (AG) v Crosbie* [1966] I.R. 426, where Ó'Dálaigh C.J. summed up the position of bail in the following terms:

> "These applicants are charged with non-capital murder and counsel for the Attorney General has given an unqualified 'no' in answer to the Court's question, 'is it apprehended that the applicants will abscond if bailed?' Nor, moreover is it apprehended that there will be any interference with witnesses. In these circumstances it is the Court's duty to admit these untried prisoners to bail."

Ó'Dálaigh C.J. also said that the only criterion or consideration for the court was whether the accused would abscond before trial or interfere with witnesses. The power to refuse bail on the basis that the accused might commit further offences was not included.

The following year, the Supreme Court revisited the issue of bail in *People (AG) v O'Callaghan* [1966] I.R. 501. In this case, a bail motion had been refused in the High Court, where Murnaghan J. set out, without reference to either *Purcell* or *Duffy*, a new and more extensive set of "matters which may be, and should be where appropriate, taken into account by the court in considering whether or not it is likely that the prisoner may evade justice".

Murnaghan J. then stated that the following were issues to which the court was entitled to have regard.

(1) The nature of the accusation/the seriousness of the charge. The heavier the charge, the greater the chance that the accused would not appear to face it.
(2) The nature of the evidence in support of the charge. The more cogent the evidence, the greater the chance of conviction and consequently the likelihood of the prisoner trying to evade justice was greater.
(3) The likely sentence on conviction; in this instance it was felt that the heavier the potential sentence, the more likely it would be that the prisoner would try to avoid it. The accused's previous record has a bearing on the probable sentence.
(4) The likelihood of more offences being committed while the accused was on bail. It was felt that a prisoner facing a long sentence would have nothing much to lose by committing further offences.
(5) The possibility of the disposal of illegally acquired property.
(6) The possibility of interference with witnesses and/or jurors.
(7) Failure to answer bail on a previous occasion.
(8) The fact that the prisoner was caught "red-handed".
(9) The objection of the AG/police authorities.
(10) The substance/reliability of the bailsmen offered.
(11) The possibility of a speedy trial.

It was also suggested that bail might be refused in order to protect the prisoner.

On appeal to the Supreme Court, Walsh J. recognised that grounds 1, 2, 3, 5, 6, 7 and 8 were acceptable, but with certain reservations. The remaining grounds were deemed not to be so. In particular, ground number 4—the likelihood of the commission of further offences while on bail—was held to be a matter which was in the view of the learned judge "quite unacceptable'. He stated that "this is a form of preventative justice which has no place in our legal system and is quite alien to the true purpose of bail".

The Supreme Court held that certain factors would be relevant in ascertaining the likelihood that the accused person would attempt to evade justice. These are as follows:

(1) The seriousness of the charge.
(2) The nature of the evidence of the accused.
(3) The likely sentence upon conviction.
(4) The likelihood that unlawfully acquired property would be disposed of/destroyed.
(5) Interference with witnesses/jurors.
(6) Previous failure to answer to bail.
(7) Whether the accused had been caught "red-handed".
(8) The objections of the AG/Gardaí.
(9) The reliability/substance of the bailsmen.
(10) The likelihood of a speedy trial.

It can be seen that most of these criteria can be categorised into two broad groups:

(1) The evasion of justice;
(2) Interference with the trial.

The Supreme Court rejected the argument that the commission of further offences in the event of bail being granted was a valid ground upon which bail could be refused.

In an attempt to deal with the situation, s.11 of the Criminal Justice Act 1984 provides for the imposition of mandatory consecutive sentences in respect of offences committed while the accused person was on bail.

In *Ryan v DPP* [1989] I.R. 399, an argument that bail could be refused in order to prevent the commission of further offences was similarly rejected. Here it had been argued that the rights of those citizens who might become victims of crime should be taken into consideration when deciding whether or not to grant bail to an accused person. The argument was rejected because, according to Finlay C.J., "the criminalising of mere intent has usually been the badge of an oppressive or unjust legal system". This remained the position until the passing of the 16th Amendment to Bunreacht na hÉireann following the Bail referendum in 1996. Article 40.4.7 of Bunreacht na hÉireann now provides that "provision may be made by law for the refusal of bail by a court to a person charged with a serious offence where it is reasonably considered necessary to prevent the commission of a serious offence by that person".

5.3 The Bail Act 1997

The Act in s.1(2) defines "serious offence" as being any crime contained in the Schedule to the Act which attracts a possible custodial sentence of five years or more for an accused person of full capacity and with no previous convictions. The court is to have regard to factors outlined in s.2(2) when deciding whether bail ought to be denied. These are broadly similar to the list of grounds laid down in *O'Callaghan,* and in addition, the court may have regard to the fact that the accused person is addicted to a controlled substance.

5.4 Refusal of Bail—Section 2 of the Bail Act 1997

Section 2 of the Bail Act provides that "where an application for bail is made by a person charged with a serious offence", bail may be refused if the court is satisfied that such refusal is "reasonably considered necessary to prevent the commission of a serious offence". For bail to be refused under s.2 of the 1997 Act, the accused must be charged with a serious offence, as defined in s.1, and the apprehended offence must also be a serious offence, although it is not required that the court be satisfied that the apprehended offence is a specific offence. Clearly though, s.2 cannot be invoked in the case of a person charged with a serious offence where the apprehended offence is of a minor nature.

If bail is refused under s.2(1) of the Bail Act, s.3 provides the accused with the right to have the application for bail renewed if his trial has not commenced within four months.

Section 4 of the Bail Act provides that where bail is being opposed under s.2, the accused's previous convictions cannot be referred to in a way that would prejudice the accused's right to a fair trial.

Section 5 of the Act relates to recognisances and provides that where bail is granted subject to recognisances, the accused person will not be released on bail until at least one third of the amount of the recognisance be paid into court.

Section 6 provides for conditions which the court may impose on bail. Failure on the part of the accused to comply with these will lead to the re-arrest of the accused and forfeiture of any recognisances.

5.5 Sentencing

Prior to the passing of the Criminal Justice Act 1984, judges were entitled to exercise discretion with regard to imposing the appropriate penalties in respect of offences committed while the accused had been on bail.

Section 11 of the 1984 Act curbed this discretion somewhat by requiring the judge to impose a consecutive sentence for such offences.

Section 11 provides that "any sentence of imprisonment passed on a person for an offence committed after the commencement of this section while he was on bail shall be consecutive on any sentence passed on him for a previous offence, or if he is sentenced in respect of two or more previous offences, on the sentence last due to expire, so however that, where two or more consecutive sentences are required by this section are passed by the District Court, the aggregate term of imprisonment in respect of those consecutive sentences shall not exceed two years."

Section 11 of the Criminal Justice Act 1984 is amended by s.10 of the Bail Act 1997. The effect of this amendment is that whereas s.11 of the 1984 Act required that mandatory consecutive sentences were imposed upon conviction for offences committed whilst on bail, s.10 of the Bail Act additionally requires that a greater sentence be imposed in respect of such offences.

It might be argued however, that both sections are rendered toothless by their failure to prevent the judge from suspending the second (or even the first) of the sentences. The Irish judiciary have traditionally been quite hostile to any intrusion by the legislature into their discretionary powers with regard to sentencing.

In *People v Noel Healy* [1989] 3 Frewen 188, the applicant was charged with a series of offences and was convicted and sentenced to concurrent terms of eight years on each count. He had been on bail when the offences were committed. When passing sentence, the judge took the total number of years which would be served into account and adjusted the sentence downwards. The applicant appealed against the severity of the sentence, arguing that he had received a much harsher punishment than had his co-accused. During the appeal, counsel for the DPP submitted that the judge should disregard the duration of the sentence imposed for a previous offence and fix a sentence appropriate to the second crime—and not follow the English practice of taking account of the total number of years to be served.

The Court of Criminal Appeal dismissed the application, holding that the sentence imposed on the accused was not excessive or founded on any error of principle, and that the comparison with the sentence handed down to the co-accused was inappropriate.

The question of suspending one of the consecutive sentences was raised in *People (DPP) v Thomas Dennigan* [1980] 3 Frewen 253, in which case the applicant pleaded guilty to a series of offences contained in two bills of indictment—the second of which referred to offences allegedly committed whilst the accused was on bail in respect of the charges contained in the first bill.

With regard to the first set of charges, the accused was convicted and sentenced to concurrent sentences, the longest of which was a term of four years. He was then sentenced to five years for the second list of offences, to run concurrently with the first term. Counsel pleaded for leniency on his behalf due to personal circumstances, and said that the court could suspend one of the sentences on the basis that nothing in the 1984 Act prevented the judge from doing so. The court held that it could suspend a consecutive sentence, but that in this case, the offences committed were too serious. The court did, however, reduce each sentence due to the fact that not enough consideration had been given to the accused's personal circumstances.

5.6 Hearsay Evidence

Following the decision of the Supreme Court in *People (AG) v McGinley* [1998] 2 I.L.R.M. 233, hearsay evidence may be adduced in support of an objection to bail under s.2 of the Bail Act. The High Court had denied bail in that case on the basis of hearsay evidence from a member of the Gardaí. On appeal, the Supreme Court held that the accused retained the right to fair procedures which included the right to test the evidence against him through cross-examination unless special factors existed which could justify the use of hearsay evidence.

No provision is made in the Act or elsewhere for the compensation of an accused person who has been denied bail and who is subsequently acquitted. Finally, bail should not be set at such a high amount as to amount to a *de facto* refusal of bail.

6. TYPES OF PUNISHMENT

Upon conviction for a criminal offence, the court must then determine the nature and severity of the punishment to be imposed. In deciding, the court will have regard to certain factors, both aggravating and mitigating, and will adjust the sentence accordingly. Aggravating factors include the level of violence used, previous convictions and where there was a serious impact on the victim. Mitigating factors include: cooperation with the Gardaí, personal circumstances of the accused and whether the accused entered a plea of guilty, particularly at an early stage.

6.1 IMPRISONMENT

Mandatory Sentences: A mandatory sentence is one which the court must impose. A conviction for murder will result in a mandatory life sentence regardless of any mitigating factors that may exist. In the case of aggravated murder, s.3 of the Criminal Justice Act 1990 provides that a conviction for aggravated murder, which essentially replaces the offence of capital murder, attracts a mandatory life sentence with the stipulation that no fewer than 40 years be served.

Section 15 of the Misuse of Drugs Act 1977 provides for a mandatory minimum sentence of 10 years in respect of a conviction under that provision. Some discretion is allowed in this case; the mandatory minimum sentence need not be imposed where the judge is satisfied that there are sufficient reasons for not imposing it.

In most other cases, sentencing is a matter for discretion of the trial judge. Sentences for multiple offences can run concurrently. This means that where, for example, an accused is being sentenced for two offences, with 12 months' imprisonment being imposed for each offence, he will spend 12 months in prison, subject to whatever amount of remission he may be entitled to. If the sentences in the example just given were ordered to run consecutively, time will start to run in respect of the second of the two sentences when the first sentence has been served. A judge can also direct that a sentence, or a part thereof, can be suspended for a specified amount of time or in the case of offences committed while on bail, sentences in respect of these must run consecutively as provided for by s.11 of the Criminal Justice Act 1984 as amended by s.10 of the Bail Act 1997.

6.2 Fines

A court may order that a convicted person may incur some financial penalty either in addition to, or instead of, a custodial sentence. The maximum amount to be imposed by the court will be laid down in the relevant Act.

6.3 Community Service Orders

The Criminal Justice (Community Service) Act 1983 provides that any court, other than the Special Criminal Court, may order an offender to carry out unpaid community work. This form of punishment is imposed in lieu of a custodial sentence on offenders older than 16 years of age. The offender must consent to the making of the order, which will stipulate the number of hours to be worked. This number of hours cannot exceed 240.

6.4 Forfeiture

The Proceeds of Crime Act 1996 makes provision for the forfeiture of property over a certain value, where the court is satisfied, on the civil standard of proof, that such property was obtained as a result of criminal activity. The Act is enforced by the Criminal Assets Bureau, set up by the Criminal Assets Bureau Act 1996. A conviction is not required prior to the confiscation of any property. In *Gilligan v Criminal Assets Bureau* [1998] 3 I.R. 185, the constitutionality of the Proceeds of Crime Act 1996 was upheld by the Supreme Court. It had been argued that the defendant's right to a trial in due course of law, as provided for by Art.38 of Bunreacht na hÉireann, had been infringed on the basis that the proceedings under the Act were of a criminal nature and that the application of the civil standard of proof was a clear violation of his Art.38 rights. This argument was rejected on the basis that the impugned provisions applied to property and not to individuals. The defendant had also argued that s.1(1) of the Act was unconstitutional on the basis that it operated retrospectively, contrary to Art.15 of Bunreacht na hÉireann, which prohibits the enactment of such legislation. The section provides that "in this Act, save where the context otherwise requires—'proceeds of crime' means any property obtained or received at any time (whether before or after the passing of this Act) by or as a result of or in connection with the commission of an offence …". This argument was also rejected on the basis that, since the possession of unlawfully obtained property hadn't been lawful prior to the passing of the Act, it could not be argued that the Act had retrospectively criminalised conduct that had been lawful.

6.5 PROBATION

The issue of probation is governed by the Probation of Offenders Act 1907. Where a person has been convicted of an offence punishable by a custodial sentence, the provisions of the 1907 Act may be invoked. There are two ways in which this might happen:

(1) Where the offender has been tried in the District Court, s.1(1) of the Act may be applied. If the District Court Judge is willing, no conviction is recorded against the offender, although the court recognises that an offence has been committed.

(2) Where the Offender has been convicted, the relevant court can order the release of the offender under s.1(2) of the 1907 Act. The Offender must however, enter into a recognisance to be of good behaviour for a period of up to three years. He will then be assigned a Probation Officer who will supervise him for the duration of his probation. Failure to abide by the terms of probation will result in the offender being sentenced for the original offence.

6.6 COMPENSATION

The Criminal Justice Act 1993 provides that courts have the power to order the payment of compensation to the victim of a crime, by the offender.

7. ELEMENTS OF A CRIMINAL OFFENCE

The component parts of a criminal offence are the *actus reus* and the *mens rea*, both of which derive from the maxim *actus non facit reum nisi mens sit rea* (An act does not make a man guilty unless his mind be also guilty). If there is no *actus reus* there is no crime and where an act is carried out in the absence of any form of guilty intention there can be no conviction. The exception to this is where an offence is one of absolute liability, where *mens rea* is irrelevant, liability being imposed on proof that the prohibited conduct had been carried out. In the vast majority of cases, both elements of the offence must be established before criminal liability can be imposed.

7.1 THE BURDEN OF PROOF

The burden of proof in a criminal trial is placed on the prosecution. This refers to what the prosecution must do in order to prove its case against the accused, and was described in the following terms in *Woolmington v DPP* [1935] All E.R. Rep 1: "throughout the web of the English criminal law one golden thread is always to be seen, that it is the duty of the prosecution to prove the prisoner's guilt ...". To discharge this burden, the prosecution must: (a) prove all the elements of the offence with which the accused is charged; and (b) disprove/negative any/all defences that are consistent with the innocence of the accused. This flows from the right of the accused to be presumed innocent until proven guilty. There are some rare exceptions to this, where the burden of proof shifts to the accused. An example is where the defence of insanity is being put forward by the accused. In this instance, it will be for the accused to prove that he was insane at the time of the commission of the offence.

7.2 THE STANDARD OF PROOF

In criminal cases, the standard of proof is "beyond reasonable doubt". This means that even where the jury believes that it is possible that the accused committed the offence with which he is charged, they must acquit him if there is a reasonable doubt in their minds as to his guilt. In *People (Attorney General) v Byrne* [1974] I.R. 1, the court stated that they must be satisfied beyond reasonable doubt that the accused committed the offence and also that the accused was entitled to the benefit of the doubt. Where, therefore, two interpretations of the accused's part in an alleged offence are possible, one being in his favour, the accused is entitled to be judged according to the more benign of the two, unless the jury is satisfied beyond reasonable doubt that the prosecution has established the contrary to the required standard. It should be remembered that "beyond reasonable doubt" does not necessarily mean "beyond all doubt". This point was clearly articulated by Denning J. in *Miller v Minister for Pensions* [1947] 2 All E.R. 372, where he stated that "proof beyond reasonable doubt does not mean proof beyond the shadow of doubt. The law would fail to protect the community if it admitted fanciful possibilities to deflect the course of justice. If the evidence is so strong against a man as to leave only a remote possibility in his favour which can be dismissed with the sentence 'of course it is possible but not in the least probable', the case is proved beyond reasonable doubt, but nothing short of that will suffice". The standard of proof is lower in civil cases, where the plaintiff must prove his case on "the balance of probabilities." Where in a criminal case the burden of proof shifts to the defence (*i.e.* insanity) this burden is discharged on the civil standard which is the balance of probabilities.

7.3 THE *ACTUS REUS*

The *actus reus* is sometimes referred to as being the physical or action element of an offence. It should be remembered however, that the *actus reus* can also include inaction or omission on the part of the accused.

Without the *actus reus*, there is no offence. It is impossible to sustain a prosecution for any offence on the basis of *mens rea* alone. In *R v Deller* (1952) 36 Cr. App. Rep. 184, the accused tried to sell a vehicle that he believed to be owned by a hire purchase company. He informed the purchaser that the car was legally his. Unknown to him, he was in fact the legal owner of the vehicle. He was acquitted of the offence of obtaining by false pretences because although he had the *mens rea* for the offence, there was no *actus reus*. As stated previously, the *actus reus* need not necessarily be a positive act on the part of the accused, and can be established where there is a "state of affairs" or where the accused has omitted to act where he otherwise should have.

7.3.1 State of affairs

In *R v Larsonneur* (1933) 29 Cox CC 673, the accused was convicted under the Aliens Order 1920, having been found in the UK. She had been sent out of the UK and had come to Ireland whereupon she was

Elements of a Criminal Offence 29

returned to the UK and handed over to the police. In *Winzar Chief Constable of Kent* (1983) (The Times, March 28, 1983), the accused was convicted of being found drunk on the highway. He had been removed from a hospital by the police and had been put into a police car which had been parked on the highway. Despite the fact that in both these cases the offences could not be said to have been due to the voluntary actions of either accused, both resulted in convictions.

7.3.2 Omission

Criminal liability for omission arises where the accused is under some form of duty to act but fails to do so. In cases where there is no duty to act, no liability for failure to act will be incurred. A duty to act can arise in different circumstances.

(1) Statutory duty. Where a duty is imposed by a statute, failure to perform the obligations imposed will amount to an offence.

(2) Contractual Duty. Where, by virtue of a contract or by virtue of holding a particular office, duties are imposed on an individual, failure to carry out those duties may lead to a conviction. In *R v Dytham* [1979] 3 All E.R. 641, a police officer who failed to act to stop a brawl was convicted of misconduct. See also *DPP v Bartley* (unreported, High Court June 13, 1997).

(3) Where the accused creates the danger, he may be convicted of an offence if he does nothing to mitigate its effects. In *R v Miller* [1983] 1 All E.R. 978, the accused was convicted of arson. He had accidentally started a fire and had done nothing to try to put it out. It was held that having started the fire, albeit by accident, he was then under a duty to extinguish it.

(4) Voluntary Assumption of Duty. There are many cases in which defendants were convicted of offences arising out of situations where they had breached a duty owed to a third party in their care. In *R v Stone and Dobinson* [1977] 2 All E.R. 341, both defendants were convicted of manslaughter where they had failed to provide medical assistance for an elderly relative of the first named defendant who had lived with them. In that case, the duty had been imposed on the first named defendant because he was related to the deceased. The duty imposed on the second named defendant had arisen because the accused had assumed a responsibility towards the

deceased. See also *R v Bubb* [1851] 4 Cox CC 455, *R v Gibbins & Proctor* [1918] 13 Cr. App. Rep.134 and *R v Taktak* [1988] 34 A Crim. R. 334.

7.3.3 Voluntariness

The action(s) of the accused must be voluntary. Accordingly, where the accused has no control over his actions, there will generally be no conviction. This is discussed further in the chapter on automatism.

7.4 THE *MENS REA*

This is the mental element of an offence. Where the accused has no *mens rea*, he cannot be convicted unless the offence is one of absolute liability. There are different degrees of *mens rea*, and will be discussed separately.

7.4.1 Intention

This category of *mens rea* can be either direct or oblique. Therefore looking at these, it is necessary to state what intention is not.

(a) Intention is not the same as motive. One's motive for committing an offence is the reason for committing it. Where there is no motive for a crime, it might be more difficult to show that the accused committed it but that does not mean that an offence has not been committed. Equally, the presence of motive may be a factor from which guilt might be easier to establish.

(b) Intention is not the same as a desire to achieve a particular result. Equally, a person can intend to carry out a particular act regardless of the likelihood that he will bring about a particular result.

7.4.2 Direct Intention

This is where the accused wanted to bring about a particular result and carried out a deliberate act in order to achieve it.

7.4.3 Oblique Intention

This form of intention is less clear-cut than direct intention and rests on what the accused foresaw as being the result of his conduct. The actions of the accused are deliberate but a result, other than the one

Elements of a Criminal Offence 31

[handwritten: Presumption of intention]

anticipated or desired, comes about. The English Courts have formulated and modified the test to be applied in cases of oblique intent and the following is a brief summary of those.

In *Hyam v DPP* [1974] 2 All E.R. 41, the defendant put burning newspaper through a letterbox causing the deaths of two children. Her motive was to frighten the owner of the house. She appealed her conviction for murder arguing that she had no intention to kill anyone. The House of Lords held that the conviction should stand if the prosecution could establish that when she had committed the act, she had known that it was highly probable that death or grievous bodily harm would result. In *R v Moloney* [1985] 1 All E.R. 1025, two men decided to compete with each other to see which of them was better at handling a shotgun. The defendant won and was then challenged by the deceased to fire the weapon. The accused duly fired and killed the deceased. In his defence, it was argued that because he was drunk, he had not considered the outcome of his actions. The House of Lords laid down a two-part test to be applied in cases such as this, and in doing so, departed from the "highly probable" test laid down in *Hyam*. The judge, in directing a jury should, where possible, avoid prescribing a definition of "intention" and leave it to the jury to decide. Where however, an explanation should be given, two questions should be posed to the jury:

(1) Was the outcome a natural consequence of the voluntary act of the accused?
(2) Was this result foreseen by the accused as being a natural consequence of his actions?

If the answer to both was yes, then the jury were entitled to infer that the accused intended to bring about the result.

In *R v Hancock and Shankland* [1986] 1 All E.R. 641, the two defendants were charged with murder having thrown a concrete slab over a bridge resulting in the death of a driver in a car on the road below. The defence argued that they did not intend to kill the deceased and that they had acted as they did in a bid to prevent miners from breaking a picket. The trial judge directed the jury in accordance with the ruling in *Moloney,* that intent could be inferred if the defendants had foreseen that death or serious injury was a "natural consequence" of their actions. On appeal, the House of Lords rejected this and held that death or serious injury had to be a probable as well as a natural consequence. The jury, therefore, ought to have been told that intent could be inferred where death or serious injury was a "natural and probable" consequence and also that the higher the probability, the more likely it was that the accused had intended the result.

In *R v Nedrick* [1986] 3 All E.R. 1, the Court of Appeal modified the test again. The facts of this case were similar to those of *Hyam*, and the jury had been directed that the accused could be convicted if he was aware that it was "highly probable" that his actions would result in someone's death. The Court of Appeal held that the jury would be entitled to infer an intention to kill or seriously injure where the defendant recognised that death or serious injury as a result of his actions, was a "virtual certainty".

Finally, in *R v Woolin* [1999] 1 A.C. 82, the House of Lords held that where a result was virtually certain, it could be viewed as being the intended result. The leading Irish case is *People (DPP) v Douglas and Hayes* [1985] I.L.R.M. 25. In that case, the defendants were appealing against their convictions for shooting with intent to kill, an offence contained in the Offences Against the Person Act 1861, on the grounds that there had been no intention to kill. The Court of Criminal Appeal followed the decision of the House of Lords in *Hyam* and held that where there was evidence that a reasonable person would have foreseen that the natural and probable consequences of the defendants' conduct was that death would result and that where it could be established that the defendants had acted recklessly, the jury was entitled to infer from that that the defendant had intended to cause death by his actions, subject to the requirement that both these facts be established beyond reasonable doubt.

7.4.4 The presumption of intent

Section 4(2) of the Criminal Justice Act 1964 provides that "the accused person shall be presumed to have intended the natural and probably consequences of his conduct, but this presumption may be rebutted". This section applies to the *mens rea* required for murder, but the presumption of intent applies to all offences in Irish law. In *People (DPP) v McBride* [1997] I.L.R.M. 233, the Court of Criminal Appeal held that the presumption of intent did not affect the presumption of innocence since it was "only a presumption and could be rebutted." In *People (DPP) v Hull* (unreported, Court of Criminal Appeal, July 8, 1996) the court held that the presumption of intent should be regarded by the jury as being a two-step process, the first step being the determination of what the natural and probable consequences of the defendant's conduct were. If the jury accepted that the natural and probable consequence of the defendant's conduct was the death of the victim, the jury was entitled to conclude that the defendant had intended that consequence. The jury would then have to deal with the second step which was to decide whether the presumption had been rebutted and that the direction of the trial judge to this effect had been correct.

7.4.5 Recklessness

This is a lesser form of *mens rea* than intention and arises where the accused has taken an unjustifiable risk. Recklessness can be objective or subjective. Subjective recklessness occurs where the accused was aware of the risk but decided to take it anyway. The leading English case on subjective recklessness is *R v Cunningham* [1957] 2 All E.R. 412, in which the court held that the test to be applied was whether the risk was in the mind of the accused. If the accused was aware of the risk and decided to take it, he was subjectively reckless in doing so. Objective recklessness occurs where the accused did not allude to the possibility that there was a risk which would have been obvious to the reasonable man. The test for objective recklessness was laid down in *Metropolitan Police Commissioner v Caldwell* [1981] 1 All E.R. 901, where the House of Lords held that the word "reckless" should be given its ordinary meaning and that where there was an "obvious risk", albeit one which was unknown to the accused, which the reasonably prudent person would have known about, the accused acted recklessly where he failed to appreciate it. The ruling in *Caldwell* was subsequently affirmed by the House of Lords in *R v Lawrence* [1981] 1 All E.R. 974. The main problem with objective recklessness as defined in *Caldwell*, was that it did not cover situations in which the accused may have considered whether or not a risk existed but decided that there was none. Equally, the application of an objective test for recklessness under *Caldwell* meant that an accused was being judged against the standard of the reasonable man even where it was manifestly unjust to the accused to do so. It was also argued that having two different forms of recklessness, each judged according to different standards, was in breach of Art.6 of the European Convention on Human Rights, which provides that anyone charged with a criminal offence is entitled to a "fair and public hearing within a reasonable time by an independent and impartial tribunal established by law". In *Elliott v C (A Minor)* [1983] 2 All E.R. 1005, the Court of Appeal upheld the conviction of a mildly mentally handicapped child who had set fire to a shed, on the basis that the risk attached to such conduct would have been obvious to the "reasonably prudent person". The effect of the so-called "Caldwell loophole" was that no distinction was drawn between the accused who had knowingly taken a risk and the accused who hadn't considered whether there was a risk at all. The House of Lords finally overruled *Caldwell* in *R v G and R* [2003] 4 All E.R. 765, where it was held that a person acts recklessly when he takes an unreasonable risk in circumstances where the risk is known to him, knowing that a certain outcome is likely. The English Courts have therefore, reverted to a subjective test.

The position in Irish law however, is not altogether clear. The decisions of the House of Lords are of persuasive authority only in this jurisdiction but it is arguable that the Irish judiciary are more flexible in their approach to various tests, (see, for example, the rules on insanity). There also appears to be a greater preference for subjective tests in the Irish courts. The leading case in this jurisdiction on recklessness is *People (DPP) v Murray* [1977] I.R. 360. The two accused were charged with capital murder and argued that they did not have the necessary *mens rea* for that offence. The question for the court was whether Mrs Murray, who had fired the fatal shot, had acted recklessly by so doing. An essential component of the offence was knowledge or recklessness on the part of the accused as to whether the victim was a member of the Gardaí. In rejecting objective recklessness, the Supreme Court (*per* Walsh J.) stated that "in this context objective recklessness is really constructive knowledge; and constructive knowledge has no place in our criminal system in establishing intent".

The decision in *Murray* raises questions as to the application of subjective recklessness in cases other than capital murder. In that case, Henchy J. stated that the *mens rea* for capital murder is subjective, without stating what the position was in relation to other offences. The same could be said of the judgments of Parke and Kenny JJ. The best that can be said is that although there appears to be a tendency towards the use of subjective tests, there are instances in which the court can apply an objective test. This can be seen in *Re Hefferon Kearns Ltd* [1993] 3 I.R. 191 and *PSS v JAS* (unreported, High Court, May 22, 1995).

7.4.6 Criminal negligence

This form of *mens rea* applies to manslaughter only and is of a higher standard than the principles of negligence under the law of tort. In *People (AG) v Dunleavy* [1948] I.R. 95, it was held on appeal that to

Elements of a Criminal Offence 35

establish negligence sufficiently grave to sustain a conviction for manslaughter, the level of negligence would have to be considerably greater than would suffice in a civil action. Criminal negligence, being a more grave form of negligence, is judged objectively.

- **Negligence**: Negligence, as a form of *mens rea*, really only arises where the offence in question requires that the accused failed to carry out some duty or acted in a way that breaches a duty. The duty in question is usually a statutory duty and negligence in this context is more akin to the concept of negligence in tort.
- **Strict Liability/Absolute Liability**: These arise where certain conduct is prohibited and is then carried out by the accused. Only the *actus reus* need be established and the *mens rea* is not relevant. In some situations, an offence of strict liability may have a defence of reasonable belief/mistake.

7.5 Coincidence of *Actus Reus* and *Mens Rea*

In order to convict someone of a criminal offence, the prosecution must not only establish the elements of that offence (*actus reus* and *mens rea*) and disprove any/all defences raised on behalf of the accused, it must also show that:

1. The *actus reus* and *mens rea* coincided; and
2. The defendant's intentional and voluntary act caused the result. This does not arise in the case of a conduct offence, the result of which is to determine the issue of imposing liability.

7.5.1 The *actus reus* and *mens rea* must coincide

Fundamentally, this means that the accused must have the *mens rea* to commit the offence in question when he is committing the *actus reus* element of the offence. Where the two do not coincide and cannot be shown to be a part of a continuing transaction, the accused will not be found guilty. A number of approaches have been formulated to deal with situations in which this problem arises.

7.5.2 Continuing act

A number of acts, separate in themselves, can nonetheless be viewed as one continuing act. *Fagan v Metropolitan Police Commissioner*

[1968] 3 All E.R. 442. The accused accidentally parked his car on a policeman's foot. When asked to remove it, he refused. He argued that *mens rea* and *actus reus* did not coincide, and that consequently, he could not be guilty of assault. The court held that the entire incident was a continuing act, the *actus reus* was already in place when the accused formed the *mens rea* for the offence by refusing to move the vehicle. A similar approach was adopted in *Kaitamaki v R* [1985] 2 All E.R. 435. In this case, the court held that rape was a continuing act beginning with penetration and ending at withdrawal. The accused had realised after penetration that there was no consent on the part of the woman but carried on. At that point, he formed the *mens rea* for rape and as the *actus reus* was already in place, his conviction for rape was upheld.

7.5.3 Duty

This approach was employed by the House of Lords in *R v Miller* [1983] 1 All E.R. 978. The accused had accidentally started a fire but did nothing to extinguish it. The Court of Appeal had upheld the conviction on the basis that it was a continuing act, having also looked at the duty approach. This approach imposes a duty on an individual to do something to mitigate the results of their conduct. Liability can then be imposed where the individual breaches that duty. The House of Lords stated that the duty approach was the better of the two in this case, on the basis that a jury would find it easier to understand.

7.5.4 The "Supposed Corpse Rule"

The clearest example of this approach is to be seen in *Thabo Meli v R* [1954] 1 All E.R. 37. The accused, believing that he had killed someone whom he had assaulted, threw the "body" over a cliff. The victim died as a result of exposure rather than from the injury caused by the initial assault. In this case, the conviction for murder was upheld on the basis that both acts were part of the one transaction. A similar decision was given in *R v Church* [1965] 2 All E.R. 72, where the Court of Appeal held that where different actions are part of the one plan, a conviction could be sustained. Clearly, when the second act is an attempt to cover up the first act, a conviction is likely.

7.5.5 Causation

In result offences, a causal link must be established between the actions of the accused and the result of those actions. In *R v White*

Elements of a Criminal Offence

[1910] All E.R. 340, the accused had administered poison to his mother but the actual cause of her death had been heart failure. In this case, the accused was convicted of attempted murder.

Whether or not a link exists between the actions of the accused and the outcome of those actions can be inferred from the surrounding circumstances. In *R v Cato* [1976] 1 All E.R. 260, the accused was convicted of manslaughter where his friend had died of an overdose of heroin. Both men were taking the drug and each man had handed the syringes to the other in order to inject the substance. Both men overdosed but the accused was saved. The Court of Appeal held that where the accused had injected the deceased and the deceased then died from the effects of the drug, a causal link had been established.

7.6 NOVUS ACTUS INTERVENIENS

This concept arises in tort as well as in criminal law and in both situations may break the chain of causation, with the result that the accused may be absolved of liability. It is essential that the causal link between the actions of the accused and the result of those actions is not broken, for liability to be imposed. Where an act by either a third party or the defendant intervenes, the chain of causation may be broken. In the case of a *novus actus* by a third party, there is the requirement that the action is voluntary. In *R v Pagett* [1983] Crim. L.R. 394, the deceased had been placed against her will, by the defendant, in the firing line of bullets fired by the police, who had been trying to arrest the accused. He appealed his conviction for murder arguing that the actions of the police amounted to a *novus actus interveniens*. This argument was rejected and the Court of Appeal also pointed out that the deceased had been placed in the situation, involuntarily, by the defendant. If the actions of the third party are calculated to protect him from the actions of the accused and where the actions by the third party are foreseeable by the accused, no *novus actus interveniens* will arise.

In addition, the actions of the third party must be unconnected to those of the accused and must amount to a new cause. In *R v Jordan* (1956) 40 Cr. App. Rep. 152, a conviction for murder was quashed. The accused had stabbed the victim causing him to be hospitalised. The victim's wound had actually almost healed but he died from pneumonia which was caused by a series of negligent acts carried out by doctors in the course of his treatment. The Court of Appeal held that the medical treatment had been "palpably wrong" and effectively held it to have been the cause of death. In *R v Smith* [1959] 2 All E.R. 193, the Court of Appeal held that where the original wound was an operating and substantial cause of death, the claim of causation would not be broken. In *R v Cheshire* [1991] 3 All E.R. 670, the Court of Appeal held that only treatment which could be described as extraordinary and unusual would amount to a *novus actus interveniens* and even then, it would have to be something that completely overshadowed the original wound.

7.6.1 The Eggshell Skull Rule

In tort, a plaintiff must take steps to mitigate his loss and failure to do so will result in a similar award of damages. This is not the case in criminal law. The accused is not entitled to expect his victim to take any steps which would lessen the effects of the accused's conduct. Equally, the accused must take his victim as he finds him and will not be able to rely on the fact that his victim suffered from some condition that renders him more susceptible to injury. In *R v Blaue* [1975] 3 All E.R. 446, the Court of Appeal refused to quash a conviction where the victim was a Jehovah's Witness and had refused a blood transfusion, necessary following an attack on her by the accused. The defendant had argued that the victim would not have died had she accepted the blood transfusion. The Court of Appeal held that the victim's injuries had been caused by the defendant and that he could not then argue that her religious beliefs were unreasonably held in order to be absolved of liability.

8. CRIMINAL LIABILITY

Criminal Liability is imposed where the prosecution discharges the burden of proving that the accused committed the *actus reus* of the offence with which he is charged and that he did so having formed the necessary level of *mens rea*. If the prosecution goes on to disprove any defences put forward by the defence, the accused will be fixed with criminal liability in respect of the offence of which he has been convicted.

8.1 Secondary Participation

These are occasions where liability is imposed on individuals other than the person who actually committed the offence, on the basis of what is called secondary participation. Secondary participation refers to any assistance given to the accused before, during or after the offence.

Traditionally, there were four categories of participation recognised by the common law and by the Accessories and Abettors Act 1861:

(1) principal in the first degree—the person who actually committed the offence.
(2) principal in the second degree—a person who aided or abetted the commission of an offence or who was present at the time of the commission.
(3) accessory before the fact—a person who provided assistance prior to the commission of the defence.
(4) accessory after the fact—a person who provided assistance to the person who committed a felony after the defence had been committed and "knowing that" a felony had been committed.

Section 8 of the Aiders and Abettors Act 1861 provided that any person who aided, abetted, counselled or procured the commission of a misdemeanour was liable to be prosecuted as a principal offender.

The Criminal Law Act 1997 repealed the older legislation and the relevant provisions are contained in ss.7 and 8 of the 1997 Act.

Section 7(1) provides that: "any person who aids, abets, counsels or procures the commission of an indictable offence shall be liable to be indicted, tried and punished as a principal offender".

In the case of summary offences, a similar provision to that contained in s.7(1) of the Criminal Law Act 1997 is to be found in s.22 of the Petty Sessions (Ireland) Act 1851.

In order to be "indicted, tried and punished" as a principal offender, an offence must actually be committed. This is also the case in respect of persons charged with summary offences. This differs from the situation in which a person is charged with an inchoate offence. An inchoate offence (attempt, conspiracy or incitement) is an offence in itself.

Both Acts refer to a person who "aids, abets, counsels or procures".

8.1.1 Aiding

To aid someone in the commission of an offence is to knowingly provide assistance in its commission. It is not required that the person providing such assistance is present at the scene of the crime.

In *Gillick v West Norfolk and Wisbech Area Health Authority* [1985] 3 All E.R. 402, it had been argued that a doctor who prescribed contraceptives for an under-age girl would be aiding and abetting in the commission of an offence. The House of Lords held that this might be the case depending on the intention of the doctor and was not dependent upon the doctor's presence at the time/location of the actual offence. Similarly, in *People (DPP) v O'Reilly* [1991] 1 I.R. 77, it was held that the provision of a vehicle for the purpose of a burglary could lead to a conviction for aiding that offence even though the accused had not actually taken part in the burglary itself.

8.1.2 Abetting

This term is more often than not used in conjunction with the term "aiding" and for all intents and purposes, appears to mean the same thing.

8.1.3 Counselling

This term refers to encouragement or advice given prior to the commission of the offence. The encouragement need not have been the cause of the offence. In *R v Calhaem* [1985] 2 All E.R. 266, the defendant told a man to kill a woman whom the accused regarded as being a "love-rival". The accused appealed against her conviction and argued that there had been no causal link between what she had said and the death of the victim. The Court of Appeal held that no causal link was required; where there had been some form of contact between the accused and the killer, this would suffice. In *R v Gianetto* [1996] Crim. L.R. 722, the trial judge stated that:

"Supposing somebody came up to (the defendant) and said 'I am going to kill your wife', if he played any part, either in encouragement, as little as patting him on the back, nodding, saying 'oh goody', that would be sufficient to involve him in the murder, to make him guilty, because he is encouraging the murder".

also incitement/conspiracy

8.1.4 Procuring

This occurs where the desired outcome is achieved through some effort on the part of the accused. In *Attorney General's Reference (No.1 of 1975)* [1975] 2 All E.R. 684, it was held that there did not have to be any agreement between the parties nor any encouragement on the part of the accused. "You procure a thing by setting out to see that it happens and taking the appropriate steps to produce that happening". (*per* Widgery L.J.)

8.1.5 *Actus Reus* of secondary participation

There must be some evidence that actual assistance was provided to the principal offender. The level of assistance need not be very high as can be seen from *R v Gianetto*, but there will be no secondary liability imposed where a person merely happens to be at the scene of a crime or fails to stop the commission of a crime. The exception to this general rule is where there is a duty to intervene and that duty is not fulfilled, as occurred in *R v Dytham*. Another exception exists where the perpetrators of the offence derive some encouragement from the presence of the accused at the scene of the crime. In *R v Clarkson* [1971] 3 All E.R. 344, it was held that for liability to be imposed in such a situation, the fact that the perpetrators of the offence were encouraged by the presence of the accused was not enough in itself. The court held that the prosecution would have to prove that the accused had intended to encourage the commission of the offence. In *People (AG) v Ryan* [1966] 1 Frewen 304, the Court of Criminal Appeal adopted the same position and in *People (DPP) v Rose* (unreported, Court of Criminal Appeal, February 21, 2002) a murder conviction was overturned on appeal on the basis that words uttered by the appellant could not be shown to have encouraged in the commission of the offence.

8.1.6 *Mens Rea* of secondary participation

It must be shown that the accessory to the offence intended to assist the principal offender and that the accessory knew that an offence was being committed by the principal offender. Intention in this context relates to encouragement or assistance in the commission of the offence. Knowledge that an offence is to be committed appears to be enough. In *DPP v Madden* [1977] I.R. 336, a conviction was upheld where the accused provided a vehicle knowing that the vehicle was to be used in a violent crime. Similarly, in *People (DPP) v Egan* [1989] I.R. 681, a conviction for robbery was upheld even though the accused did not know that an armed robbery had been planned. Liability was imposed on the basis that he had provided the robbers with a place to store a vehicle that had been used in the commission of the offence knowing that a "small stroke" was to take place.

A victim of an offence will not be convicted as an accessory despite the fact that they could be said to "facilitate" or encourage its commission. An example would be where a man is charged with incest under the Punishment of Incest Act 1908. The female in that situation will not be deemed to be an accomplice, particularly in view of the fact that the Act seeks to protect people from being victims of the offence.

Section 7(2) of the 1997 Act provides that where a person, knowing that an arrestable offence has been committed, acts with the intention of preventing the arrest of a guilty party, he is guilty of an offence.

8.2 The Doctrine of Common Design (Joint Enterprise)

Although there are similarities between the doctrine of common design and secondary participation, the main difference is that under the doctrine of common design, where two or more agree to commit an offence, each party is a principal offender; whereas secondary participants are complicit in offences carried out by principals. In the former, all parties are principal offenders whereas in the latter the parties are dealt with as though they were principal offenders.

This however, would appear to be becoming more of an academic or theoretical distinction rather than a practical one. *Dicta* from various judgments of the Court of Criminal Appeal suggest that the judiciary regard the two concepts as being interchangeable. In *R v Anderson and Morris* [1996] 2 All E.R. 644, the Court of Appeal held that "where two persons embark on a joint enterprise, each is liable for the acts done in pursuance of that joint enterprise, that includes unusual consequences if they arise from the execution of the agreed joint enterprise but ... if one of the adventurers goes beyond what has been tacitly agreed as part of the common enterprise, his co-adventurer is not liable for the consequences of that unauthorised act".

The main point to be taken from that definition is that where there is an agreement to carry out an offence, all parties to that agreement are liable. But where one party goes further then what was agreed and does something else that was not foreseeable to the other parties, then they are not liable for this unsanctioned activity.

The issue of foresight was also discussed in *Chang Wing-Siu v R* [1985] A.C. 168, where the three accused, armed with knives, set about committing a robbery, during which, a person was stabbed and later died as a result. The accused were each charged with murder and their defence was that although they had brought knives along in order to carry out the robbery, there had been no intention to use them. Their argument was that the knives had been used in self-defence and that neither accused had foreseen the actual use of the knives. The trial judge directed the jury that if the defendants had foreseen serious bodily harm or death as a possibility, this would be enough to convict them even where they did not intend the eventual outcome. On appeal, it was held that the trial judge's direction had been correct and that where the prosecution could show that the use of the weapon was foreseen by the defendants as being a real possibility, this would suffice for a conviction for murder arising from a joint enterprise. This is so even where it would have to be established that the actual killer must have had the required *mens rea* for murder. In *People (DPP) v Murray* [1977] I.R. 360, the defendants, a married couple, were involved in a bank robbery. They were pursued by Gardaí and Mrs Murray shot and killed a Garda. Both were convicted of capital murder. On appeal, the Supreme Court held that there had been a common design in relation to the robbery and to the use of violence and also with regard to murder, but that there was no common design with regard to capital murder because there was no evidence to suggest that they had agreed on the use of violence against the Gardaí.

However, in both *People (DPP) v Pringle* [1981] 2 Frewen 57 and *People (DPP) v Eccles* (unreported, Court of Criminal Appeal, February 10, 1986) the Court of Criminal Appeal found that there had been a common design in respect of capital murder. The difference between these cases and the *Murray* case is that in *Pringle* and *Eccles*, there had been some evidence of the intention to overcome the Gardaí using whatever force was necessary, whereas no such evidence existed in *Murray*.

In *People (DPP) v Doolan* [2002] 4 I.R. 463, the accused had hired another man to carry out a punishment beating but told him not to shoot the victim. The victim died from shotgun wounds to the leg. The defence argued that the joint enterprise went no further than the punishment beating and that the use of the shotgun had been outside the scope of the original agreement. The court applied *R v Anderson and Morris* and concluded that there had been a common design and that it had been agreed that the victim would suffer serious injury. That being enough to prove murder, the use of the gun, even though it had not been sanctioned, was not outside the scope of common design.

8.2.1 Withdrawal from complicity

If an accessory calls off the arrangement before the crime is committed, they will not be liable for any offences carried out after they have withdrawn. It was held that the withdrawal should be communicated to the other participants, and in *R v Jensen and Ward* [1980] VR 1904, it was held that withdrawal should either be communicated or that some positive step should be taken, such as calling the police.

8.3 VICARIOUS LIABILITY

At common law, no one can be held liable for the crimes of another. This was pointed out in *Hardcastle v Bielty* [1982] 1 QB 709. There are some instances arising mainly out of an employer/employee relationship where an employer may be liable for the criminal acts of his employee, where the employee is acting within the scope of his employment. The issue can also arise under the Intoxicating Liquor Acts.

8.4 STRICT LIABILITY

These offences are mostly statutory offences with the exceptions of the common law offences of public nuisance and criminal libel. Where a strict liability offence is created by statute, the wording used will indicate the level of *mens rea* required. Until recently s.1 of the Criminal Law Amendment Act 1935 provided for the offence of statutory rape. This offence required proof of *mens rea* for the first two parts of the *actus reus, i.e.* (i) sexual intercourse, (ii) with a female, (iii) who is under the age of 17, the third part of the *actus reus* did not require any *mens rea*, the man's knowledge or belief regarding the female's age being irrelevant.

8.5 ABSOLUTE LIABILITY

These offences require no *mens rea* whatsoever and are complete when the *actus reus* is committed. An example of this type of offence had been contained in s.1(1) of the Criminal Law (Amendment) Act 1935; this section was held by the Supreme Court to be unconstitutional in CC v Ireland (2006).

8.6 CRIMINAL LIABILITY OF CORPORATIONS

At common law, a corporation could not be held criminally liable, notwithstanding the fact that they are viewed as persons by the law. Practical considerations also applied—not all penal sanctions could be imposed on a corporation.

However, it is possible to impose criminal liability on a corporate entity in some situations. To determine corporate liability for criminal acts, the question to be answered was whether the act was carried out by someone who had control within the company, such as would enable him to direct the activities of the company. In *Tesco Supermarkets v Nattrass* [1972] A.C. 153, the House of Lords held that a regional manager employed by the plaintiff company could not be regarded as senior enough within the company to enable him to direct the mind and will of the company. A corporation cannot be held liable for the fraudulent acts of employees where the fraud is perpetrated against the company itself. This was held in *Canadian Dredge and Dock Co. v R* [1985] I.S.C.R. 662. It need hardly be said that there are certain crimes which are incapable of being committed by a company, *e.g.* bigamy, but there are a number of so-called "corporate crimes" which are governed by legislation. Section 8 of the Environmental Protection Agency Act 1992 and s.11 of the Air Pollution Act 1997 are two examples of statutory provisions that impose criminal liability on companies for offences under those Acts. In *Alphacell Ltd v Woodward* [1972] A.C. 824, the House of Lords had to decide whether, for the purposes of the offence in question, which involved pollution of a river, the defendant had to have intended to cause the pollution. It was held that this was not necessary; liability for the pollution could be established by showing that the pollution was caused by the defendant. The word "cause" was to be given its ordinary meaning and the House of Lords essentially held that but for the activities of the defendant, the pollution would not have occurred. This was enough to impose liability for the offence in question. A similar reasoning was used by the Supreme Court in *Maguire v Shannon Regional Fisheries Board* [1994] 2 I.L.R.M. 253. However, in *Shannon Regional Fisheries Ltd v Cavan County Council* [1996] 3 I.R. 267, Keane J., in a dissenting judgment, stated that there were some offences which necessitated the establishment of *mens rea*. Where the only punishment for an offence is a custodial sentence, a company cannot be convicted of it.

8.7 Transferred Intent

There are situations where liability may be imposed even where the actual victim of the defendant's action is not his intended target. In these situations, the defendant's malice towards his intended victim is deemed to have been transferred to his actual victim. In *R v Latimer* (1886) 16 Cox CC 70, the defendant had intended to hit one person but missed, hitting and injuring another person instead. He appealed his conviction on the basis that he had not meant to injure the actual victim. His conviction was upheld on the grounds that his malicious intent had been transferred from his intended target to the injured party. The doctrine of transferred intent is also provided for in some statutory provisions; s.4(1) of the Criminal Justice Act 1964 provides that "where a person kills another unlawfully the killing shall not be murder unless the accused intended to kill, or cause serious injury to, *some person, whether the person actually killed or not*." (my emphasis). Similar provisions are to be found in s.6 of the Non-Fatal Offences Against the Person Act 1997 in relation to syringe offences.

The doctrine does not apply in situations where there is no similarity between the *mens rea* for the intended offence and that which is required for an actual offence with which the defendant is charged.

9. HOMICIDE

The term "homicide" denotes the unlawful killing of a human being. The circumstances of any particular case, coupled with the level of *mens rea* on the part of the accused will determine whether the homicide is murder, manslaughter or infanticide. Suicide is no longer a criminal offence in this jurisdiction, having been abolished by s.2(1) of the Criminal Law (Suicide) Act 1993. Aiding and abetting the suicide of another remains an offence under s.2(2) of that Act.

9.1 Murder

Murder has always been an offence at common law. The most often quoted common law definition of murder is that of Chief Justice Coke:

> "Murder is when a man of sound memory, and at the age of discretion, unlawfully killeth within any country of the realm any reasonable creature *in rerum natura* under the King's peace with malice aforethought either expressed by the party or implied by law, so as the party wounded, or hurt, etc. die of the wound, or hurt, etc. within a year and a day of the same."

The common law definition still holds true, with a number of modifications. First, the *mens rea* for murder is now contained in s.4 of the Criminal Justice Act 1964 which provides in s.4(1) that:

> "Where a person kills another unlawfully the killing shall not be murder unless the accused intended to kill, or cause serious injury to, some person, whether the person actually killed or not."

Section 4(2) provides that:

> "The accused person shall be presumed to have intended the natural and probable consequences of his conduct, but this presumption may be rebutted."

Secondly, it is no longer the case that the death has to occur within a year and a day of the injury. The so-called "year and a day rule" was abolished by s.38 of the Criminal Justice Act 1999.

Thirdly, the common law definition requires that the accused be "of sound memory, and of the age of discretion". This simply means that the accused must be sane and over the age of criminal responsibility, which is currently seven years of age in this jurisdiction.

Finally, the requirement at common law that the victim be "any reasonable creature *in rerum natura*" means that the victim must have been a human being, born alive.

9.1.1 Causation

Murder is a result offence and therefore it must be shown that the accused caused the unlawful death. Where the link between the accused's conduct and the victim's death is broken by a *novus actus interveniens*, the accused will not be liable.

9.1.2 Attempted murder

In order to prove the charge of attempted murder, the prosecution must show that the accused carried out the *actus reus* with the intention to kill. The accused cannot be convicted of attempted murder if the *mens rea* was the intention to cause serious injury.

9.1.3 Penalty on conviction

Murder is an indictable offence and carries a mandatory sentence of life imprisonment.

9.1.4 Aggravated murder

The offence of aggravated murder is contained in s.3 of the Criminal Justice Act 1990. The aggravating factor is the identity of the victim or where the killing is carried out in the course of the commission of certain offences under the Offences Against the State Act 1939. The section applies to the following categories of people:

- A member of the Garda Síochána acting in the course of his duty; or
- A prison officer acting in the course of his duty; or
- The Head of a foreign State, a member of the government of a foreign State or a foreign diplomat, where the murder is committed in this State in furtherance of a political objective. Section 3 of the 1990 Act also applies to attempts to carry out any such murders.

Homicide 49

This offence replaces the offence of capital murder which was an offence punishable by death. The death penalty was abolished by s.1 of the Criminal Justice Act 1990 and s.4 of that Act provides that the penalty for aggravated murder is a mandatory life sentence with the specification that a minimum term of 40 years be served.

9.2 MANSLAUGHTER

Manslaughter is a common law offence and arises in two ways:

9.2.1 Voluntary manslaughter

Where the accused has committed the *actus reus* for murder and has the *mens rea* for that offence but successfully pleads either provocation or excessive self-defence, he will be acquitted of murder but convicted of manslaughter. This is because these two defences are partial defences which reduce the offence from murder to manslaughter. An acquittal will never be justified since, by definition, the accused has committed the *actus reus* of murder with the necessary *mens rea*. The justification for the reduction of the offence to manslaughter is that the *mens rea* was caused by the action(s) of the deceased. From the point of view of the accused, the main benefit of this reduction is that the mandatory life sentence is avoided, leaving the penalty to be decided by the judge.

9.2.2 Involuntary manslaughter

Involuntary manslaughter occurs where the accused does not have the *mens rea* for murder, but where the victim dies as a result of the actions or sometimes the omissions of the accused. There is, therefore, no *mens rea* for manslaughter *per se*; the offence occurs where, but for the availability of either provocation or excessive self-defence (voluntary manslaughter), the accused would be convicted of murder or where the actions of the accused lead to the unintended death of the victim (involuntary manslaughter). Liability for involuntary manslaughter can arise in any one of three different ways.

9.2.3 A criminal and dangerous act

The leading case on this type of manslaughter in this jurisdiction is *People (AG) v Crosbie and Meehan* [1966] I.R. 490, where the Court of Criminal Appeal held that in order to sustain a conviction for manslaughter, the act causing the death of the victim had to be unlawful and dangerous. The issue of whether an act is dangerous is for the jury to decide. In *People (DPP) v Hendley* (Court of Criminal Appeal, June 11, 1993), the Court of Criminal Appeal held that in addition to the requirement that the act causing death be unlawful and dangerous, it was also necessary to show that it had been deliberate.

9.2.4 Criminal negligence

This occurs where an otherwise lawful act is performed with such a high level of negligence that any reasonable person would have been aware that it carried a substantial risk of serious injury. In *R v Adomako* [1994] 3 All E.R. 79, the House of Lords held that in order to decide whether the accused had been criminally negligent, the jury had to ask a number of questions:

(i) Was there negligence as that term is understood in the context of civil law?
(ii) Was the victim's death caused by the negligence of the accused?
(iii) In acting as he did, did the accused deviate considerably from the standard of care which would have been expected of him?

Where these questions were answered in the affirmative, the accused could be convicted of manslaughter.

In *People (AG) v Dunleavy* [1948] I.R. 95, the Court of Criminal Appeal held that the jury should be told that a very high degree of negligence had to be established in the case of manslaughter. The test is objective and the accused's subjective belief in the reasonableness of his actions is irrelevant. Similarly, in *People (DPP) v Cullagh* (unreported, Court of Criminal Appeal, March 15, 1999), it was stated that the negligence of the accused had to be shown to be "gross negligence" and that the ordinary standard of negligence in civil cases could not be enough to sustain a conviction for manslaughter.

9.2.5 Breach of duty

Where the accused refuses or neglects to fulfil a duty that is imposed on him—by virtue of a contract, a statute, his relationship with the victim, his office or by his own assumption of a duty to care for the victim—a conviction for manslaughter may result where the victim dies as a result of that breach of duty by the accused. In *R v Instan* [1893]

17 Cox CC 602, the accused refused to provide food or medical assistance for an elderly relative with whom she lived. This refusal led to the death of the victim and the accused was convicted of manslaughter. Similarly in *R v Stone and Dobinson* [1977] 2 All E.R. 341, convictions for manslaughter were returned where the two accused had failed to provide medical help for a dependant relative who lived with them. The court held that in the case of the first defendant, the duty had arisen from his blood relationship to the deceased and in the case of the second defendant, the duty had arisen because the second defendant had taken it upon herself to carry out certain tasks for the deceased. Once this responsibility had been accepted, a duty had been assumed by the second defendant and that breach of duty resulted in a conviction for manslaughter. See also *R v Senior* (1899) 19 Cox CC 219 and *R v Taktak* (1988) 34 A. Crim. R. 334.

9.2.6 Penalty on conviction

The penalty is at the judge's discretion.

9.3 INFANTICIDE

The offence of infanticide is a very narrowly defined one and is provided for by the Infanticide Act 1949. Section 1 of the Act creates the offence, which is the killing of an infant (under one year of age), through an act or omission that would otherwise be murder, by the mother of the infant who, at the time of the offence was suffering from the effects of pregnancy, childbirth and/or lactation, with the result that her mind was adversely affected. The offence is a recognition that a woman may well be suffering from physical and emotional/psychological ill-effects of pregnancy and childbirth, but is illogical in the sense that the offence only applies to the killing of a child under the age of one year.

9.3.1 Penalty on conviction

Section 6(3) of the Criminal Law (Insanity) Act 2006 provides that "a woman found guilty of infanticide may be dealt with in accordance with subsection (1)." Section 6 of the 2006 Act provides for diminished responsibility. The 2006 Act is dealt with in the *Chapter on Insanity*. Prior to the passing of the 2006 Act, the penalty for a woman convicted of infanticide was left to the discretion of the court and was dealt with as manslaughter.

9.4 EUTHANASIA

Section 2(2) of the Criminal Law (Suicide) Act 1993 renders it an offence to aid, abet, counsel or procure a suicide or an attempted suicide by another person. This is the case even though neither suicide nor attempted suicide is an offence. Nonetheless, any person who intentionally kills another is guilty of murder and his motivation for doing so, however well-intentioned, is irrelevant as is the "consent" of the victim. It is not unlawful to withdraw or withhold medical treatment even where to do so will result in death. Where a patient refuses medical treatment or requests that it be discontinued and the patient is of sufficient capacity to make that decision, such a request must be acceded to. In *Re a Ward of Court (Withdrawal of Medical Treatment)* [1996] 2 I.R. 79, the Supreme Court held that the so-called "right to die" is regarded as being a corollary of the constitutionally protected right to life and an expression of the unenumerated rights of bodily integrity (*Ryan v AG* [1965] I.R. 294) and privacy (*McGee v AG* [1974] I.R. 284 and *Kennedy v Ireland* [1987] I.R. 587).

10. SEXUAL OFFENCES

The law in relation to sexual offences has traditionally condemned three types of sexual conduct: sexual activity carried out in the absence of the consent of one of the parties, sexual conduct carried out where one of the parties lacks capacity to give legal consent and that which, although engaged in consensually, was deemed to be inherently wrong on the basis that it was repugnant to traditional moral standards. Rape is the clearest example of the first of these categories, but despite the moral and legal condemnation it attracted, a man could not be convicted for raping his wife until the "marital rape exemption" was abolished by the Criminal Law (Rape) (Amendment) Act 1990. Nor could a man be raped until the passing of that Act.

The law in relation to the second type of sexual conduct has also undergone a radical change following the recent Supreme Court decision in *CC v Ireland & Ors* [2006] I.E.S.C. 33, which struck down as unconstitutional s.1(1) of the Criminal Law Amendment Act 1935 on the basis that a man charged with unlawful carnal knowledge of a girl under the age of 15 years did not have a defence of reasonable mistake available to him. In *A v The Governor of Arbour Hill Prison* [2006] I.E.H.C. 169, the applicant, who had been charged, tried and convicted of the offence which had been struck down by the Supreme Court in *CC v Ireland & Ors,* challenged the legality of his continued detention in respect of the offence. His application was granted by the High Court and he was duly released from custody. This decision was subsequently overruled by the Supreme Court and the applicant was then rearrested. The written decision of the Supreme Court was not available at the time of writing. The Criminal Law (Sexual Offences) Act 2006 was rushed through the Oireachtas in the wake of the case of "Mr A" and the offences contained within it are applicable to both sexes. Finally, the law has also traditionally criminalised activity which, even when carried out by consenting adults, was deemed sufficiently harmful to the moral fabric of society to warrant criminal sanction. The most obvious example of this category of offence was the offence of buggery which had been covered by ss.61 and 62 of the Offences Against the Person Act 1861. This offence was abolished by s.3 of the Criminal Law (Sexual Offences) Act 1993. This chapter looks at the main offences of a sexual nature covered by Irish law.

10.1 Rape

Section 2(1) of the Criminal Law (Rape) Act 1981 provides the statutory basis for what is still referred to as "common law rape". Rape is committed where a man has sexual intercourse with a woman, who at the time of the intercourse does not consent and where the man either knows that the woman does not consent or is reckless as to whether or not she consents.

> The *actus reus* of rape is having sexual intercourse with a woman who does not consent.
> The *mens rea* is knowledge of, or recklessness as to the absence of the woman's consent.

Rape under the 1981 Act is a gender-specific offence which can only be carried out by a man against a woman. Until the passing of the Criminal Law (Rape) (Amendment) Act 1990 a man could not be convicted of raping his wife due to the requirement at common law that sexual intercourse had to be "unlawful", and since this meant outside marriage, husbands were granted a "marital rape exemption". Section 5 of the Criminal Law (Rape) (Amendment) Act 1990 abolished this requirement, although the consent of the DPP is still required before a prosecution for rape within marriage can be brought. Another exemption existed in respect of boys under the age of 14 who were conclusively presumed to be incapable of rape. This presumption has been abolished by s.6 of the 1990 Act and consequently, a boy under the age of 14 (but older than seven) may be prosecuted, provided that the presumption of *doli incapax* has been rebutted.

For the purposes of s.2(1) of the 1981 Act, sexual intercourse means vaginal intercourse only. The offence is complete upon penetration which must be proven. In *People (AG) v Dermody* [1956] I.R. 307, it was held that the slightest penetration would suffice.

10.1.1 Consent

Absence of the woman's consent is part of the *actus reus* and this must be established. Consent must be freely given and where consent is subsequently withdrawn, the man must desist or he may be liable to a charge of rape. The same applies where the man realises that there is no consent on the part of the woman. In *Kaitamaki v R* [1984] 2 All E.R. 435, it was held that rape was a continuing act and that the accused was guilty of the offence when he continued having intercourse after he had become aware that the woman did not consent.

10.1.2 Vitiating factors

Consent may be vitiated where it is induced by fraud. In *R v Flattery* (1877) 13 Cox CC 388 and in *R v Williams* [1922] All E.R. 433, convictions for rape were returned where the consent of the complainants had been induced by fraudulent misrepresentations as to the nature of the act. The complainant in the first case had been told that she was having a surgical procedure carried out and the complainant in the second case had been told that she was undergoing a procedure that would improve her singing voice. The fraudulent misrepresentation must be in relation to the nature of the act of sexual intercourse. In *R v Linekar* [1995] 3 All E.R. 69, the accused was acquitted of raping a prostitute. She had agreed to have intercourse with him in return for a specified sum of money which was then not paid. There was evidence that indicated that the accused had no intention of paying. This however did not amount to fraud for the purpose of gaining consent to sexual intercourse. The complainant had agreed to have intercourse with the accused and the fact that he made off without paying her did not have any relevance to the issue of consent.

The woman must be capable of giving consent. In *R v Mayers* (1872) 12 Cox CC 311 and in *People (DPP) v X* (unreported, Court of Criminal Appeal, 1995), it was held that a sleeping woman was incapable of giving consent. Similarly, consent may be vitiated where it is induced by intoxication. In *R v Camplin* [1845] 1 Cox CC 220, the accused was convicted of rape where he had caused the complainant to become intoxicated and then had sexual intercourse with her. In *R v Lang* [1975] 62 Cr. App. Rep. 50, the Court of Appeal held that it is the effect of the intoxicant on the complainant and not the fact that she consumed it that is relevant and that where a woman is incapable of exercising judgment due to intoxication, consent will not be valid.

Failure to resist is not the same as consent. Section 9 of the Criminal Law (Rape) (Amendment) Act 1990 provides that failure to offer resistance does not of itself constitute consent. The jury is entitled to take this matter into account and may infer consent where no evidence of resistance is adduced.

10.1.3 Submission

Submission to sexual intercourse is not the same as consenting to it. Where the complainant submits to intercourse due to fear or intimidation, consent is not freely given. In *R v Olugboja* [1981] 3 All

E.R. 443, it had been argued by the defence that the complainant had been "persuaded" to have sexual intercourse with the accused. The Court of Appeal held that a jury in a rape trial should be told that consent and submission are not the same and that while every consent involves submission, the reverse is not always true.

10.1.4 *Mens Rea*

As previously stated, the *mens rea* for rape, as with most sexual offences, is the man's knowledge of the woman's absence of consent or his recklessness to that fact. In the situation where a man believes that the woman is consenting, the question arises as to whether an honest belief is enough or whether it must also be reasonable. Section 2(2) of the 1981 Act states that where this issue is raised, the jury is to have regard to the presence or absence of reasonable grounds for the defendant's belief. The test has both subjective and objective elements; the defendant's honest belief is relevant but the jury must then determine whether the defendant had any reasonable grounds upon which to base his belief. This approach was eventually adopted in England following the decision of the House of Lords in *DPP v Morgan* [1975] 2 All E.R. 347. In that case, the House of Lords held that an honest belief, however unreasonably held, meant that an accused could not be convicted of rape. In this jurisdiction, the jury in a rape trial need only be directed as to the provisions of s.2(2) if the accused claims that he believed that the woman was consenting. This is clear from the wording of the provision itself and was held to be the case by the Supreme Court in *People (DPP) v McDonagh* [1996] 1 I.R. 565.

10.1.5 Recklessness

The test for recklessness is likely to be subjective. In *People (DPP) v Creighton* [1994] 1 I.L.R.M. 551, the Court of Criminal Appeal stated that recklessness was the same as heedless conduct. The test in English law is subjective. In *R v Satnam and Kewel* [1988] Crim. L.R. 236, the Court of Appeal held that where the defendant had continued having intercourse regardless of the woman's consent, the jury was entitled to conclude that he had acted recklessly.

10.1.6 Penalty on conviction

Rape is an indictable offence and is punishable by a maximum sentence of life imprisonment.

10.2 Rape under Section 4 of the Criminal Law (Rape) (Amendment) Act 1990

This section deals with offences of a penetrative nature other than that covered by s.2 of the Criminal Law (Rape) Act 1981. Unlike rape under the 1981 Act, the offences covered by s.4 of the 1990 Act are drafted in gender-neutral terms and can therefore be committed by a man against either a man or a woman and *vice versa*. The *actus reus* is the penetration of the mouth or anus by a penis or the penetration of the vagina with a hand-held object without the consent of the complainant.

The *mens rea* is not stated in the section itself, but given that an offence under s.4 is one of sexual assault, albeit one which involves penetration, it makes sense to regard the *mens rea* for sexual assault as being applicable, with the same being the case in relation to the issue of consent.

10.2.1 Penalty on conviction

Rape under s.4 is an indictable offence and is punishable by a maximum sentence of life imprisonment.

10.3 Sexual Assault

Section 2 of the 1990 Act gives statutory expression to the common law offences of indecent assault upon a male person and indecent assault upon a female person. Both offences are now combined in a gender-neutral form in the section. The *actus reus* of sexual assault is the same as that for the offence of assault under s.2 of the Non-Fatal Offences Against the Person Act 1997 with the additional requirement that it be carried out in circumstances of indecency. This means that two things must be established: assault plus circumstances of indecency. Assault occurs where the accused either intentionally or recklessly directly or indirectly applies force to the body of the complainant or where the accused causes the complainant to reasonably fear that he will be subjected to immediate physical contact to which he does not consent. Consent, therefore, is a defence to a charge of sexual assault, provided of course that consent is freely given by a person with the capacity to give it.

The second element of the *actus reus* is that the assault must take place in circumstances which are indecent. What amounts to indecency will depend on the facts of each case but where there is uncertainty, the guidelines laid down by the House of Lords in *R v*

Court [1988] 2 All E.R. 221, may be of some assistance. In that case, the House of Lords categorised different types of conduct under three headings:

(i) Acts that are not inherently indecent. An example might be where the accused removes someone's coat. This is not an inherently indecent act and the fact that the accused derives some form of gratification from doing it will not suffice to render it an indecent act.
(ii) Acts that are inherently indecent, regardless of the motive of the accused. These will suffice for the purpose of establishing circumstances of indecency.
(iii) Acts that may be indecent depending on the circumstances. In determining whether these acts are indecent, the jury should have regard to how they might be viewed by right-minded people, taking the relationship between the parties and the reason for the accused's actions into consideration.

10.3.1 Penalty on conviction

Sexual Assault under s.2 of the 1990 Act is an indictable offence carrying a maximum term of five years' imprisonment.

10.4 AGGRAVATED SEXUAL ASSAULT

Section 3 of the 1990 Act deals with the offence of aggravated assault. Essentially, this is a more serious form of the offence under s.2 of the Act and comprises sexual assault coupled with the use or threat of serious violence, grave humiliation, degradation or injury. The *actus reus* has two elements: the intentional assault in circumstances of indecency and the use or threat of serious violence, grave humiliation, degradation or injury. There are also two parts to the *mens rea*: the intention to commit an indecent assault and the intention to use or threaten to use serious violence, grave humiliation, degradation or injury.

Consent may not be a defence to an offence under s.3 of the 1990 Act. The section envisages activity of a much graver nature than that which is contemplated by s.2. An analogy might be drawn with s.4 of the Non-Fatal Offences against the Person Act, which creates the offence of Causing Serious Harm. Consent is not a defence to that offence and it seems reasonable to suppose that given the nature of the offence under s.3 of the 1990 Act, as reflected by the potential penalty attracted by it, that consent would not be a defence to a charge of aggravated sexual assault either. In *R v Brown* [1993] 2 All E.R. 75, the House of Lords refused to allow a defence of consent to charges of assault causing actual bodily harm. The case involved a group of sado-masochists who had inflicted injuries—some of which required hospitalisation—on each other. The defendants argued that they had participated in the conduct consensually and that their convictions should be overturned. When the House of Lords ruled against them, they brought a case before the European Court of Human Rights, arguing that their rights under the European Convention on Human Rights had been breached. In *Laskey, Jaggard and Brown v UK* [1997] 24 E.H.R.R. 59, the European Court of Human Rights held against the applicants stating that the defendant had the right and the duty to protect vulnerable sectors within society and that this did not breach any right asserted by the applicants under the Convention.

10.4.1 Penalty on conviction

Aggravated Assault is an indictable offence and carries a maximum sentence of life imprisonment.

10.5 STATUTORY RAPE

A girl who is under the age of consent (17 years) cannot, by definition, give consent to sexual intercourse. Therefore, regardless of the girl's willingness to engage in sexual intercourse, no defence of consent can avail the accused. The legislation governing this issue was, until recently, the Criminal Law Amendment Act 1935, s.1(1) of which provided that the unlawful carnal knowledge of a girl who is under the age of 15 was an offence regardless of any purported consent on the part of the girl and regardless of the belief on the part of the man that the girl was older than 15. Section 2 of the 1935 Act provided that the unlawful carnal knowledge of a girl between the ages of 15 and 17 was also an offence, albeit a less serious one. Consent on the part of the girl was irrelevant as was the belief on the part of the man that the girl was older than 17. In effect, these offences were offences of absolute liability; all that had to be established was that sexual intercourse had taken place. Section 1(1) of the 1935 Act was struck down by the Supreme Court as being repugnant to the terms of Bunreacht na hÉireann in *CC v Ireland & Ors* [2006] I.E.S.C. 33, on the basis that an accused didn't have any defence of honest mistake available to him. In response to the Supreme Court's ruling, the Oireachtas passed the Criminal Law (Sexual Offences) Act 2006. Section 2 of the Act replaces s.1(1) of the 1935 Act with a similar provision but provides in s.2(3) that "it shall be a defence to proceedings for an offence under this section for the defendant to prove that he or she honestly believed that, at the time of the alleged commission of the offence, the child against whom the offence was alleged to have been committed had attained the age of 15 years." Where the accused relies on the defence of honest mistake, the Act provides that the court shall have regard to the presence or absence of reasonable grounds for such belief. Although the only provision struck down as being repugnant to the terms of Bunreacht na hÉireann was s.1(1) of the 1935 Act, s.1(2)—which provided that the attempted defilement of a girl under the age of 15—and s.2—which provided for similar offences in respect of girls between 15 and 17—were repealed by s.3 of the Criminal Law (Sexual Offences) Act 2006. The new offences are drafted in gender-neutral terms and consequently, apply to offences against males as well as females. The defence of honest mistake is similarly available to these offences.

10.5.1 Penalty on conviction

An offence under s.2 of the 2006 Act is an indictable offence and is punishable by a maximum sentence of life imprisonment.

An offence under s.3 of the 2006 Act is an indictable offence and is punishable by a maximum sentence of five years or, in the case of an accused person who is in a position of authority as defined by the Act, to a maximum sentence of 10 years' imprisonment. Where the accused is convicted of attempting to commit an offence under s.3, the maximum sentence is two years' imprisonment or, in the case of an accused who is in a position of authority, four years' imprisonment.

Provision is made in the Act for heavier penalties in cases where the accused has previous convictions under the Act.

10.6 SEXUAL OFFENCES AGAINST MENTALLY ILL PERSONS

Section 5 of the Criminal Law (Sexual Offences) Act 1993 creates the offences of:

(1) Intercourse with a mentally impaired person or an attempt to have intercourse with a mentally impaired person.

(2) Buggery or attempted bugger of a mentally impaired person.
(3) Acts or attempted acts of gross indecency by a male against a male who is mentally impaired.

Mental impairment is defined in s.5 as "suffering from a disorder of the mind, whether through mental handicap or mental illness which is of such a nature or degree as to render a person incapable of living an independent life or of guarding against serious exploitation".

10.6.1 Defences

(1) Marriage—where the accused is married to the mentally impaired person or has reasonable grounds to so believe, no offence is committed.
(2) Lack of knowledge—where the accused did not know and had no reason to suspect that the person was mentally impaired, the accused will have a defence on this basis.

The jury must also have regard to the accused's state of mental health and where the accused is of limited intelligence, this factor should be borne in the minds of the jury.

10.7 OFFENCES BETWEEN MALES

Following the decision of the European Court of Human Rights in *Norris v Ireland* [1991] 13 E.H.R.R. 186, the Oireachtas passed the Criminal Law (Sexual Offences) Act 1993. Under the provisions of the 1993 Act, the offence of buggery, as contained in s.61 of the Offences Against the Person Act 1861, was abolished, thereby decriminalising this form of sexual activity between consenting male adults. Section 3 of the 1993 Act contained offences of buggery against males under the age of 15 and between 15 and 17 respectively. This section has now been repealed by ss.2 and 3 of the Criminal Law (Sexual Offences) Act 2006.

10.7.1 Penalty on conviction

An offence under s.2 of the 2006 Act is an indictable offence and is punishable by a maximum sentence of life imprisonment.

An offence under s.3 of the 2006 Act is an indictable offence and is punishable by a maximum sentence of five years or, in the case of an accused person who is in a position of authority as defined by the

Act, to a maximum sentence of 10 years' imprisonment. Where the accused is convicted of attempting to commit an offence under s.3, the maximum sentence is two years' imprisonment or, in the case of an accused who is in a position of authority, four years' imprisonment.

Provision is made in the Act for heavier penalties in cases where the accused has previous convictions under the Act.

10.8 Gross Indecency

Section 11 of the Criminal Law (Amendment) Act 1885 provided that it was an offence to commit or attempt to commit any act of gross indecency, whether in public or in private. The Act provided no definition for "gross indecency", but essentially the offence amounted to sexual activity between males, excluding buggery. Section 11 of the 1885 Act had been repealed by s.4 of the Criminal Justice (Sexual Offences) Act 1993 which provided that it was an offence to commit or attempt to commit acts of gross indecency with males under 15 years of age or with males between 15 and 17. This too has been repealed by ss.2 and 3 of the 2006 Act.

10.8.1 Penalty on conviction

As above.

10.9 Incest

The Punishment of Incest Act 1908 makes it an offence to engage in sexual intercourse with someone who is closely related by blood. Consent is not a defence.

10.9.1 Incest by a male

Incest by a male is committed where a man has sexual intercourse with a woman who is to his knowledge his mother, sister, half-sister, daughter or granddaughter. The offence is not committed if there is no blood relationship between the accused and the woman.

10.9.2 Incest by a female

Incest by a female is committed where a woman over the age of 17 permits her father, grandfather, brother, half-brother or son to have sexual intercourse with her, knowing that they are related by blood.

For the purposes of the offence of incest, sexual intercourse is vaginal intercourse only.

10.10 THE SEX OFFENDERS ACT 2001

The Sex Offenders Act 2001 contains a number of provisions which impose certain obligations on individuals convicted of any of the sexual offences to which the 2001 Act applies. The obligations imposed by the Act exist alongside any penal sanction imposed by the court in respect of such offences and the Act provides for the length of time for which these obligations are effective. Part 2 of the Act imposes obligations on sex offenders to provide the Gardaí with certain information concerning their name, home address or any other address used by them. Sex offenders convicted in another jurisdiction are also amenable to the provisions of the Act. Part 3 of the Act provides for Sex Offenders Orders which are granted on the application of a member of the Gardaí, not below the rank of Chief Superintendent, where the court is satisfied that the Order should be granted in order to protect the public. The Order prohibits the person named within it from carrying out certain types of conduct specified in the Order.

11. NON-FATAL OFFENCES AGAINST THE PERSON

Prior to the enactment of the Non-Fatal Offences Against the Person Act 1997, the law in relation to non-fatal offences was contained primarily in the Offences Against the Person Act 1861. The 1861 Act contained many specifically defined offences and was often criticised for being overly technical. The Non-Fatal Offences Against the Person Act 1997 modernised the law in relation to these types of offences and also created certain new offences.

11.1 ASSAULT

The offence of assault is contained in s.2(1) of the 1997 Act. Section 2(1) provides that an assault is committed where the defendant, without lawful excuse and without consent, intentionally or recklessly:

(a) directly or indirectly applies force to or causes an impact upon the body of another; or
(b) causes another to believe on reasonable grounds that he or she is likely to be immediately subjected to the direct or indirect application of such force or impact.

Section 2 therefore encompasses the common law offence of assault which is now contained in s.2(1)(b) and battery which is provided for by s.2(1)(a).

The *actus reus* is the direct or indirect application of force or causing an impact to the body of another or causing the other person to believe on objectively reasonable grounds that the application of such force or the causing of such impact is imminent. The absence of the victim's consent is also a part of the *actus reus*.

The *mens rea* is intention or subjective recklessness.

11.1.1 Consent

Consent may be either express or implied. No offence under s.2 will be committed where:

(i) the defendant did not know or believe that his conduct was unacceptable to the other person; or
(ii) the force was not intended to injure and was unlikely to do so; or

(iii) the conduct is no more that what is to be expected as part of everyday life.

11.1.2 Words as a form of assault

Section 2 of the Act is silent on the issue of whether mere words can amount to an assault. Clearly, words would not suffice for s.2(1)(a). At common law, words were not capable of constituting an offence unless they were accompanied by some threatening gesture. In *Tuberville v Savage* (1669) 1 Mod. Rep.3, words were held to negative an assault where the accused had put his hand on his sword and told the victim that "if it were not assize time, I would not take such language". In effect, the accused had told the victim that he was not going to assault him. It would seem that words would suffice to constitute an assault under s.2(1)(b).

11.1.3 Force

Section 2(2) of the Act defines "force" and provides that force includes the application of heat, light, electric current, noise or any other form of energy or the application of matter in any form.

11.1.4 Immediacy

The victim must believe that the direct or indirect application of force will be immediately forthcoming.

11.1.5 Punishment on conviction

Assault under s.2 of the 1997 Act is a summary offence only and is punishable by a maximum sentence of six months' imprisonment and/or a maximum fine of €1904.61 (£1,500).

11.2 ASSAULT CAUSING HARM

Section 3 of the 1997 Act provides that "a person who assaults another, causing him or her harm shall be guilty of an offence". Harm is defined in s.1 of the Act as being "harm to the body or mind and includes pain and unconsciousness".

The *actus reus* of a s.3 offence has two components, both of which must be established. It must be shown that the accused has committed an assault as defined in s.2 and that harm, as defined in s.1, has resulted. In *R v Ireland* [1997] 4 All E.R. 225, the House of Lords held that an assault causing actual bodily harm had been committed by the accused where a number of his victims had suffered psychological trauma as a result of receiving threatening letters that he had sent.

The *mens rea* of an offence under s.3 of the 1997 Act is intention or subjective recklessness. Section 3 itself does not state this, but given that an offence under s.3 is essentially the same as an offence under s.2 with the added requirement that harm be shown, the *mens rea* of a s.3 offence can be implied from the wording of s.2.

11.2.1 Punishment on conviction

An offence under s.3 may be tried summarily or on indictment. On summary conviction the penalty is a maximum term of imprisonment of 12 months and/or a maximum fine of €1904.61 (£1,500). On conviction on indictment, the penalty is a maximum term of imprisonment of five years and/or an unlimited fine.

11.3 Causing Serious Harm

Section 4 of the 1997 Act provides that "a person who intentionally or recklessly causes serious harm to another shall be guilty of an offence". "Serious harm" is defined in s.1 as being "an injury which creates a substantial risk of death or which causes serious disfigurement or substantial impairment of the mobility of the body as a whole or of the function of any particular bodily member or organ".

The *actus reus* of this offence is causing serious harm. It is not necessary to prove the elements of an assault for the purposes of s.4. In many cases, the level and nature of the injury sustained will imply an assault but it is important to note that assault is not a part of the *actus reus* of an offence under s.4.

The *mens rea* is intention or subjective recklessness. The accused must have *mens rea* with regard to the dangerous conduct and to the likelihood that serious harm would be caused by it.

11.3.1 Consent

Absence of consent is an integral part of the *actus reus* of an offence under s.2, and by implication under s.3. Since it is not necessary to show that an assault has taken place to establish the *actus reus* of an offence under s.4, the question arises as to whether consent may be a defence to such an offence. It would appear that consent is not generally a defence to serious harm but there may be exceptional circumstances in which it might amount to a defence. The caselaw suggests that public policy considerations will take precedence over the individual's consent. The case of *R v Brown* [1993] 2 All E.R. 75, has already been discussed in the context of sexual offences, but is also relevant to a discussion of consent in the context of serious harm.

11.3.2 Punishment on conviction

An offence under s.4 is tried on indictment and carries a maximum penalty of life imprisonment and/or an unlimited fine.

11.4 THREATS TO KILL OR CAUSE SERIOUS HARM

Section 5 of the Act provides that "a person who, without lawful excuse, makes to another a threat, by any means intending the other to believe it will be carried out, to kill or cause serious harm to that other or a third person shall be guilty of an offence".

The *actus reus* of this offence is making a threat to kill or cause serious harm. The method of making such a threat is irrelevant.

The *mens rea* is the intention to make the threat coupled with the intention that the victim believes that the threat will be carried out.

There are both similarities and differences between this offence and that of assault. If a threat is made that is capable of being immediately carried out, an offence under both sections has been committed provided that the threat is to kill or cause serious injury. One difference between the two offences is that whereas an assault centres around the immediacy of the threat, an offence under s.5 does not. Another difference is that for an assault to take place, the victim must believe that the application of force is imminent, whereas an offence under s.5 is committed regardless of the actual belief of the victim. What matters is that the accused *intended* the victim to believe that the threat will be carried out.

11.4.1 Punishment on conviction

An offence under s.5 may be tried summarily or on indictment. On summary conviction the penalty is a maximum term of imprisonment of 12 months and/or a maximum fine of €1904.61 (£1,500). On conviction on indictment the penalty is a maximum term of imprisonment of 10 years and/or an unlimited fine.

11.5 Syringe Offences

Sections 6, 7 and 8 of the 1997 Act create various offences involving the use of syringes. It is arguable that the inclusion of syringe offences in an Act originally intended to streamline the existing legislation defeats that purpose somewhat, since the conduct prohibited by these provisions criminalises the *modus operandi* of carrying out activities that were not lawful to begin with. An analogy might be drawn with the various offences relating to the criminal damage to property contained in the Criminal Damage Act 1991. Section 14(1) of the Criminal Damage Act 1991 provides that where any of the offences contained in s.2 of that Act are committed by means of fire, this will be an aggravating factor which will attract a higher penalty. Arguably, the same could have been done in the Non-Fatal Offences Against the Person Act 1997 in respect of offences carried out using syringes.

Section 1 of the 1997 Act provides definitions relevant to the offences contained in the Act. "Syringe" is defined as including "any part of a syringe or a needle or any sharp instrument capable of piercing skin and passing onto or into a person blood or any fluid or substance resembling blood". "Contaminated blood" and "contaminated fluid" are also defined and a "contaminated syringe" is one which has "in it or on it contaminated blood or contaminated fluid".

11.6 Syringe Attacks

Section 6(1) provides that it is an offence to injure another by piercing the skin of that other person with a syringe or threatening to do so, intending the victim to believe that it is likely that he may become infected with a disease.

The *actus reus* is piercing the victim's skin with a syringe or threatening to do so.

The *mens rea* is intention or subjective recklessness in relation to the piercing or the threat thereof, coupled with intention or objective recklessness in relation to causing the victim to believe that he has been infected with a disease.

11.6.1 Punishment on conviction

This offence may be tried summarily or on indictment. On summary conviction the maximum penalty is a prison sentence of 12 months and/or a maximum fine of €1904.61 (£1,500). On conviction on indictment the maximum penalty is a term of imprisonment of 10 years and/or an unlimited fine.

11.6.2 Spraying blood or a blood-like substance

Section 6(2) provides that it is an offence to pour, put or spray blood or a blood-like substance onto another person or to threaten to do so, intending the victim to believe that he may become infected with a disease.

The *actus reus* is spraying, putting or pouring blood or a blood-like substance on to the victim or threatening to do so.

The *mens rea* for this offence is intention or recklessness in relation to the spraying, putting or pouring of blood or a blood-like substance onto the victim coupled with the intention of causing the victim to believe that he may become infected or being objectively reckless as to whether the victim will so believe.

11.6.3 Punishment on conviction

This offence may be tried summarily or on indictment. On summary conviction the maximum penalty is a prison sentence of 12 months and/or a maximum fine of €1904.61 (£1,500). On conviction on indictment the maximum penalty is a term of imprisonment of 10 years and/or an unlimited fine.

11.6.4 Transferred intent

Section 6(3) provides that where in the course of committing an offence under either of the two previous sections, the actual victim is a third party, the doctrine of Transferred Intent will apply and the accused, if convicted, will be liable for the penalties provided for by the relevant sections.

11.6.5 Stabbing with a contaminated syringe

The offences contained in s.6(5) of the 1997 Act are aggravated forms of syringe offences. Section 6(5)(a) creates the offence of intentionally injuring another person by piercing his skin with a contaminated syringe.

The *actus reus* of the offence is stabbing with a contaminated syringe.

The *mens rea* is the intention to pierce the skin with a syringe and knowledge of the fact that the syringe is contaminated.

Section 6(5)(b) makes it an offence to spray, put or pour contaminated blood onto another person.

The *actus reus* is spraying, putting or pouring contaminated blood onto another person. It would appear therefore that to spray, pour or put contaminated fluid, other than blood, is an offence under s.6(2) but not under s.6(5).

The *mens rea* is intention.

Section 6(5)(c) provides for liability for the above offences arising out of transferred intent.

11.6.6 Punishment on conviction

Section 6 offences are tried on indictment and the maximum penalty is life imprisonment.

11.6.7 Possession and abandonment of syringes

Section 7 of the 1997 Act makes it an offence to possess a syringe or any blood in a container in any place with the intention of using it unlawfully to threaten or injure or intimidate another person. The section gives the Gardaí the power to stop, question and if necessary, search a person where the Garda has reasonable grounds for believing that the person is in possession of the relevant articles with the intention of using them to injure, threaten or intimidate. Failure to co-operate with the Garda or obstruction of the Garda is an offence under the section. It will be a defence to show that the syringe or container is in the possession of the accused for a valid reason.

11.6.8 Punishment on conviction

If tried summarily, the offence of failing to co-operate or obstructing the Garda carries the maximum penalty of a term of imprisonment of six months and/or a fine of €1904.61 (£1,500).

The punishment for the substantive offence of possession on summary conviction is a maximum term of imprisonment of 12 months and/or a fine of €1904.61 (£1,500); on indictment the maximum penalty is a maximum sentence of seven years and/or an unlimited fine.

Section 8 of the Act deals with the placement or abandonment of syringes in any place where it is likely that injury will be caused and is caused, or where it is likely to frighten another person. It will be a defence to show that the person in possession of the syringe has a valid reason for such possession. Where the syringe is found in the defendant's normal place of residence and the defendant did not intentionally leave it in such a place or a manner that it was likely to cause or did cause injury, this will also amount to a defence.

11.6.9 Punishment on conviction

On summary conviction the maximum penalty is a term of 12 months' imprisonment and/or a fine of €1904.61 (£1,500) and on conviction on indictment the maximum penalty is a term of seven years and/or an unlimited fine.

Where the accused is convicted on indictment of an offence under s.8(2), which is the intentional placement of a contaminated syringe in such a manner that it injures another, the maximum penalty is life imprisonment.

11.7 COERCION

Section 9 of the 1997 Act makes it an offence to engage in conduct with the objective of compelling the victim to do or to abstain from doing that which the victim is lawfully entitled to do or abstain from doing. The prohibited conduct includes violence, intimidation, damage to property, watching or besetting certain places frequented by the victim and following the victim.

11.7.1 Punishment on conviction

On summary conviction the maximum penalty is a term of 12 months' imprisonment and/or a fine of €1904.61 (£1,500) and on conviction on indictment the maximum penalty is a term of five years and/or an unlimited fine.

11.8 HARASSMENT

The offence of harassment is provided for by s.10 of the 1997 Act and occurs where the accused persistently follows, watches, besets or communicates with the victim. The type of behaviour envisaged by the section is that which is commonly referred to as "stalking". The offence is committed where the accused "by his or her acts intentionally or recklessly, seriously interferes with the other's peace or privacy and causes alarm, distress or harm to the other." The accused's actions must be intentional or reckless but the essence of the offence is the effect that those acts have on the victim. To this end the actions must be "such that a reasonable person would realise that the acts would seriously interfere with the other's peace and privacy, or cause alarm, distress or harm".

11.8.1 Punishment on conviction

On summary conviction the maximum penalty is a term of 12 months' imprisonment and/or a fine of €1904.61 (£1,500) and on conviction on indictment the maximum penalty is a term of five years and/or an unlimited fine.

Additionally, the court may impose a "non-contact" order. Section 10(3) permits the court to make such an order which is similar to an injunction in its effects. The order may prohibit certain conduct by the accused and failure to comply with the order is an offence in itself. The court, under s.10(5), is permitted to make such an order even where the accused has not been convicted of the offence, if the court is satisfied that to do so would be in the interests of justice. In *People (DPP) v Ramachandran* [2000] 2 I.R. 307, the accused had successfully appealed his conviction for harassment. Despite this, the court granted a "non-contact" order against him on the basis that his victims were in need of the court's protection.

11.9 DEMANDS FOR PAYMENT

Under s.11 of the 1997 Act, it is an offence to make demands for payment of a debt by methods which amount to misrepresentation, fraud or where the demands are intended to cause distress, alarm or humiliation to the victim by virtue of their frequency.

11.9.1 Punishment on conviction

This is a summary offence which carries a maximum fine of €1904.61 (£1,500).

11.10 POISONING

Section 12 provides that "a person shall be guilty of an offence if, knowing that the other does not consent to what is being done, he or she intentionally or recklessly administers to or causes to be taken by another a substance which he or she knows to be capable of interfering substantially with the other's bodily functions".

This includes a substance which could cause sleep or unconsciousness. The offence is committed either by directly administering a substance or causing the victim to take it. The offence therefore encompasses the "spiking" of drinks.

11.10.1 Punishment on conviction

On summary conviction the maximum penalty is a term of 12 months' imprisonment and/or a fine of €1904.61 (£1,500) and on conviction on indictment the maximum penalty is a term of three years and/or an unlimited fine.

11.11 ENDANGERMENT

Section 13 provides that it is an offence for a person to intentionally or recklessly engage in conduct which creates a substantial risk of death or serious harm to another. In *People (DPP) v Mc Grath* (unreported, Court of Criminal Appeal, May 27, 2004) and *People (DPP) v Cagney* (unreported, Court of Criminal Appeal, May 27, 2004) convictions for endangerment were upheld. In *McGrath,* the conduct in question was running after the victim and threatening him and in *Cagney* the defendant had struck the victim, causing him to fall and sustain injury. A separate offence of Endangering Traffic is contained in s.14. This offence is committed by intentionally placing any dangerous obstruction on a road, railway, street, etc., being aware that injury to a person or damage to property may be caused by doing so or being reckless as to that fact.

11.11.1 Punishment on conviction

Both offences can be tried summarily or on indictment. On summary conviction the maximum penalty is a term of 12 months' imprisonment and/or a fine of €1904.61 (£1,500) and on conviction on indictment the maximum penalty is a term of seven years and/or an unlimited fine.

11.12 FALSE IMPRISONMENT

The offence of false imprisonment is contained in s.15 of the 1997 Act, which abolishes the common law offences of kidnapping and false imprisonment. Section 15(1) provides that a person shall be guilty of false imprisonment if he:

(a) takes or detains; or
(b) causes to be taken or detained; or
(c) otherwise restricts the personal liberty of another person.

The absence of consent on the part of the victim is a part of the *actus reus* of the offence. Section 15(2) provides that where the consent of the victim has been obtained by force, threat of force or deception, causing the victim to believe that he is legally obliged to consent, this will not amount to consent on the part of the victim.

11.12.1 Punishment on conviction

On summary conviction the maximum penalty is a term of 12 months' imprisonment and/or a fine of €1904.61 (£1,500) and on conviction on indictment the maximum penalty is life imprisonment.

11.13 CHILD ABDUCTION

The issue of child abduction is covered by ss.16 and 17 of the 1997 Act. Section 16 makes it an offence for a parent or guardian to remove a child from the jurisdiction in violation of a court order or without the consent of the other parent or guardian(s). The accused will have a defence if he was unable to obtain the consent of any other parties whose consent should have been obtained, but acted in the belief that such consent would have been forthcoming. The accused can also rely on the defence that it was not his intention to deprive the other parent or guardian(s) of their rights.

Section 17 deals with the abduction of children by anyone other than the categories of persons covered by s.16. In this case there is no requirement that the child be removed from the jurisdiction. The essence of the offence is the intention to take or detain or cause to be taken or detained, a child younger than 16 years of age so that the child is removed from the custody of the person(s) who has or have control of the child. The accused will have a defence if he believes that the child is over the age of 16 years.

11.13.1 Punishment on conviction

Both offences can be tried summarily or on indictment but the DPP must consent to proceedings being taken in respect of the offence contained in s.16.

On summary conviction the maximum penalty is a term of 12 months' imprisonment and/or a fine of €1904.61 (£1,500) and on conviction on indictment the maximum penalty is a term of seven years and/or an unlimited fine.

12. OFFENCES AGAINST PROPERTY

This chapter looks at offences relating to criminal damage to property and at offences of dishonesty. The former is governed by the provisions of the Criminal Damage Act 1991 and the latter by those of the Criminal Justice (Theft and Fraud Offences) Act 2001.

12.1 THE CRIMINAL DAMAGE ACT 1991

The Criminal Damage Act 1991 repealed most of the pre-existing common law and statutory rules in relation to criminal damage to property. Section 2 the 1991 Act creates three categories of offence: Damaging Property, Damaging Property with the Intent to Endanger Life and Damaging Property with Intent to Defraud. Offences involving threats to damage property, possession of anything with the intent to damage property and unauthorised accessing of data are also contained in the Act.

For the purposes of the Act, "property" is defined in s.1 as being either tangible or in the form of data. "Damage" is also defined in s.1 and includes destruction, defacing, rendering inoperable and also altering, corrupting and doing any act contributing to such alteration of data.

12.1.1 Lawful excuse

Section 6 of the 1991 Act provides for the defence of lawful excuse where the defendant honestly believed that the owner of the property had or would have consented to the damage or where the defendant believed that causing damage to property was necessary in order to protect himself or another person or property from immediate harm and where the defendant believed that such action on his part was reasonable. This second application of the defence has been amended by s.21 of the Non-Fatal Offences Against the Person Act 1997, which requires that the actions of the defendant in damaging property have to be objectively reasonable in the circumstances.

12.2 DAMAGING PROPERTY

Section 2(1) of the 1991 Act provides that "a person who without lawful excuse damages any property belonging to another intending to damage any such property or being reckless as to whether any such property would be damaged shall be guilty of an offence".

The *actus reus* is causing damage to someone else's property without having lawful excuse for doing so.

The *mens rea* is intention or recklessness as to whether damage is caused.

The actual owner of the property need not be identified and further, s.7(2) provides that two presumptions arise in the context of damage to property. First, it is presumed that the property does belong to another person and secondly, it is presumed that the owner of the property did not consent to the damage caused. The first presumption may be rebutted by showing that on the balance of probabilities, the property belongs to the defendant and the second presumption may be rebutted, again on the balance of probabilities that the owner did consent to the damage.

12.3 Damaging Property with Intent to Endanger Life

This offence is contained in s.2(2) of the Act and is an aggravated form of the offence contained in the previous section. The aggravating factor is the intent to endanger life. Section 2(2) provides that:

> "a person who, without lawful excuse damages any property, whether belonging to himself or another –
> (a) intending to damage any property or being reckless as to whether any property would be damaged; and
> (b) intending by that damage to endanger the life of another, or being reckless as to whether the life of another would be thereby endangered, shall be guilty of an offence."

The *actus reus* is essentially the same as that required in s.2(1) but differs in respect of the question of ownership of property, which is irrelevant to the offence under s.2(2).

The *mens rea* has two aspects. First, the accused must intend to damage the property or be subjectively reckless as to whether such damage is caused. Secondly, the accused must intend to endanger life or be subjectively reckless as to whether life is endangered by the damage.

12.4 Damaging Property with Intent to Defraud

This offence is contained in s.2(3) which provides that "a person who damages any property, whether belonging to himself or another with intent to defraud, is guilty of an offence".

The *actus reus* is damaging any property. In common with s.2(2), the issue of ownership of the property is irrelevant.

The *mens rea* has two components. First, there must be the intent to damage the property. Secondly, the accused must intend by his actions to defraud others. Actual fraud need not be established.

12.5 Arson

The common law offence of arson is abolished by s.14(1) of the 1991 Act. Where damage under any offence contained in s.2 is caused by fire, such offence will be treated as arson.

12.5.1 Punishment on conviction

The offences contained in s.2 may be tried summarily or on indictment. On summary conviction the maximum penalty is a term of imprisonment of 12 months and/or a fine of €1,270 (£1,000).

On conviction on indictment the maximum penalty for an offence under s.2 is a term of imprisonment of 10 years and/or a fine of €12,697 (£10,000). Where a person is guilty of arson under ss.2(1) or 2(3), the maximum penalty is life imprisonment and/or an unlimited fine. The maximum penalty for the offence contained in s.2(2) is life imprisonment and/or an unlimited fine whether the offence is caused by arson or not.

12.6 Threats to Damage Property

It is an offence under s.3 of the Act to threaten, or without lawful excuse to damage property owned by another person or to threaten to damage one's own property in circumstances where it would be likely to endanger the life of another person. The essence of the offence is the threat to damage property; if the threat is carried out, the matter will be dealt with under the appropriate part(s) of s.2.

12.6.1 Punishment on conviction

On summary conviction the maximum penalty is a term of imprisonment of 12 months and/or a fine of €1,269.74 (£1,000). On conviction on indictment, the maximum penalty is a sentence of 10 years' imprisonment and/or a maximum fine of €12,697.38 (£10,000).

12.7 Possession with Intent to Damage Property

Under s.4 of the 1991 Act, it is an offence to have in one's custody or under one's control, without lawful excuse, any implement that is intended to be used to commit an offence under s.2.

12.7.1 Punishment on conviction

On summary conviction the maximum penalty is a term of imprisonment of 12 months and/or a fine of €1,269.74 (£1,000). On conviction on indictment the maximum penalty is a sentence of 10 years' imprisonment and/or a maximum fine of €12,697 (£10,000).

12.8 Unauthorised Accessing of Data

Section 5 of the 1991 Act creates the new offence of unauthorised accessing of data. This offence relates to the activity commonly referred to as "hacking". The offence is committed where a person within this jurisdiction "hacks" into a computer which is either within the State or outside it. It is also an offence for someone outside the State to use a computer to access any data kept within the State. It appears that the potential scope of this provision is very broad. The offence is committed where a computer is used with the intent to access data; it is not committed when data is actually accessed. Potentially, therefore, an offence under s.5 is committed where the computer user even inadvertently types in the wrong password to access online material such as email.

12.8.1 Punishment on conviction

An offence under s.5 is a summary offence and carries a maximum penalty of three months' imprisonment and/or a maximum fine of €634.86 (£500).

12.9 Theft and Dishonesty

12.9.1 The Criminal Justice (Theft and Fraud Offences) Act 2001

The Criminal Justice (Theft and Fraud Offences) Act 2001 repealed the Larceny Acts 1861, 1916 and 1990 and the Forgery Acts 1861 and 1913, which had previously governed the area of dishonesty. The 2001 Act consolidates and streamlines the offences contained in the older Acts and creates new offences relating to white-collar and computer crime.

12.9.2 Theft

Section 4 provides that "a person is guilty of theft if he or she dishonestly appropriates property without the consent of its owner and with the intention of depriving its owner of it."

The *actus reus* of theft is the appropriation of property without the consent of its owner.

The *mens rea* is the intention to deprive the owner of the property.

12.9.3 Dishonesty

"Dishonesty" is defined in s.2(1) as being "without a claim of right made in good faith". The test here is subjective. In *People (DPP) v O'Loughlin* [1979] I.R. 85, the Court of Criminal Appeal held that were there was an honest belief on the part of the accused as to whether he had a right to take property belonging to someone else, such belief would amount to a claim of right even where the belief turned out to be mistaken.

Under s.4(4) of the 2001 Act, the jury should have regard to the presence or absence of reasonable grounds for the belief.

Section 4 differs significantly from the provision of the Larceny Act 1916 on the issue of appropriation. Whereas the 1916 Act required the accused to have taken and carried away the property, the 2001 Act provides that appropriation may occur even were the accused has possession of property belonging to another person. Appropriation is defined as "usurping or adversely interfering with the proprietary rights of the owner".

It is not necessary, under s.4, to show that the accused intended to permanently deprive the owner of his property. This is another significant departure from the older legislation which required proof of an intention to permanently deprive.

12.9.4 Consent

Consent is a defence to a charge of theft. Section 4(2) of the 2001 Act provides that property is not appropriated without the consent of the owner in the following circumstances:

(a) the accused believes that he has or would have the owner's consent if the owner knew about the appropriation of the property;
(b) the accused believes that the owner cannot be ascertained by taking reasonable steps.

The belief on the part of the accused is taken subjectively but under s.4(4), the jury is to have regard to the presence or absence of reasonable grounds for his belief. The defence is lost where it is obtained by intimidation or fraud.

12.9.5 Property

Section 2(1) defines property, and includes money and real or personal property. Section 5 deals with situations involving appropriation of real property. Generally, land cannot be stolen and the term land includes anything that forms part of the land or anything that is affixed to the land.

There are three exceptions to this general rule and they are found in s.5(2) which provides that:

(1) where the defendant has a duty imposed upon him by virtue of his being a trustee, a personal representative, the liquidator of a company or someone with power of attorney and he appropriates land in breach of his duty; or

(2) where the defendant appropriates anything that forms part of the land by severing it or causing it to be severed, while not being in possession of the land; or

(3) where the defendant possesses the land under a tenancy agreement or a lease and appropriates any fixture or structure; such appropriations will amount to theft.

12.9.6 Punishment on conviction

Theft is an indictable offence which carries a maximum sentence of 10 years and/or an unlimited fine.

12.9.7 Making gain or causing loss by deception

Sections 6, 7 and 8 of the Act deal with the offences of making gain or causing loss by deception, obtaining services by deception and making off without payment, respectively.

12.9.8 Punishment on conviction

These are all indictable offences and offences under ss.6 and 7 are punishable by a maximum term of imprisonment of five years and/or an unlimited fine. The offence of making off without payment under s.8 carries a maximum sentence of two years and/or a fine of €3,809.21 (£3,000).

12.9.9 Unlawful use of a computer

This is a new offence created by s.9 of the 2001 Act. It amplifies the provisions of s.5 of the Criminal Damage Act 1991, which created the offence of unauthorised accessing of data or "hacking". The type of action contemplated by s.9 is deemed to be more serious in nature than the "hacking" offence prohibited by s.5 of the 1991 Act and requires evidence that the accused made unlawful use of a computer, either within the State or outside the State, with the intention of making a gain for himself or causing a loss to another.

12.9.10 Punishment on conviction

This is an indictable offence which carries a maximum sentence of 10 years and/or an unlimited fine.

12.9.11 False accounting

Section 10 of the 2001 Act makes it an offence to destroy, deface, conceal or falsify accounts or documents pertaining to accounts, with the intention to make a gain or to cause a loss to another. It is also an offence under s.10 to make false or misleading accounts.

False accounting is an indictable offence which carries a maximum sentence of 10 years and/or an unlimited fine.

12.10 BURGLARY

Section 12 provides that the offence of burglary is committed where a person enters a building as a trespasser with the intent to commit an arrestable offence, or being present as a trespasser, commits or attempts to commit an arrestable offence. An arrestable offence is defined in s.12(4) as being an offence "for which a person of full age and not previously convicted may be punished by imprisonment for a term of five years or by a more severe penalty".

The *actus reus* of burglary is entry on to premises as a trespasser to commit an arrestable offence or being on the premises as a trespasser and committing or attempting to commit such an offence.

There are two aspects to the *mens rea*: first, the accused must have the *mens rea* to enter the premises as a trespasser. It must be shown that he either intended to trespass or was reckless as to whether he was trespassing. Secondly, the accused must have the *mens rea* for the arrestable offence.

12.10.1 Trespass

Trespass is the unauthorised entry on to the property of another. It can happen in a number of ways:

(i) where the accused knowingly enters the premises without consent.
(ii) where the accused has permission to be on the premises but then acts in a way that is not compatible with that permission.
(iii) where the accused, having entered the premises innocently, subsequently realises that he is trespassing and fails to leave.

12.10.2 Entry

Section 12(2) provides the definition of "building" or "part of a building". For the purposes of the offence of burglary, entry does not necessarily have to mean full entry. In *R v Brown* [1985] Crim. L.R. 212, it was held that where the accused had partially entered a shop through a broken window this constituted a sufficient entry.

12.10.3 Punishment on conviction

Burglary is an indictable offence which carries a maximum term of imprisonment of 14 years and/or an unlimited fine.

12.11 AGGRAVATED BURGLARY

This offence is covered by s.13 and occurs where the offence of burglary (s.12) is committed by the accused who has with him or has at the time, a firearm, imitation firearm, any weapon of offence or an explosive.

12.11.1 Weapon

For the purposes of the Act, s.13(2) provides definitions of the types of weapons referred to in s.13(1).

A firearm is defined as including the following:

- a lethal firearm or any weapon capable of discharging a shot, bullet or other missile;
- an airgun or any other weapon which incorporates a barrel and which is capable of firing metal or other slugs;
- a crossbow; or any type of gun which emits energy and causes shock or other disablement.

An imitation firearm is anything that is not a firearm, but which resembles one.

A weapon of offence is any article with a sharp blade or point, any other article made or adapted to cause injury or incapacitation or any weapon of any description that is designed to emit any noxious substance.

The *actus reus* of aggravated burglary is essentially the same as with burglary but includes the possession of a weapon at the material time.

The *mens rea* is the same as for burglary with the added requirement that the accused knew that he had a weapon.

12.11.2 Punishment on conviction

Aggravated burglary is an indictable offence which carries a maximum sentence of imprisonment for life.

12.12 ROBBERY

The offence of robbery is provided for by s.14 of the 2001 Act. A person commits robbery when he steals, and at the time or immediately before the stealing, and in order to do so, he or she uses force or puts or seeks to put any person in fear of being then and there subjected to force.

The *actus reus* of robbery has two separate components:

(i) stealing
(ii) the use of force or threat of force at the time of the stealing or immediately prior to the stealing.

The use or threat of force need not be directed at the owner of the property. The use or threat of force must be immediately prior to or at the time of the stealing. It is not, therefore, robbery to take someone's property and *then* subject them to force or threaten to do so. The essence of the offence is the use or threat of force in order to facilitate the stealing.

The *mens rea* also has two components: first, the accused must have the intention to steal and secondly, the accused must intend to use force or threaten to use force in order to steal.

12.12.1 Punishment on conviction

Robbery is an indictable offence which carries a maximum sentence of imprisonment for life.

12.13 HANDLING

Section 17 provides that the offence of handling is committed where a person, knowing that property is stolen, or reckless as to that fact, receives it or undertakes to assist in its retention, removal, disposal or realisation.

The *actus reus* of handling is receiving stolen property and assisting in its removal, disposal or realisation.

The *mens rea* is knowledge of or recklessness as to whether the property is stolen.

Recklessness is defined by s.16(2) and can be established where the accused has ignored or disregarded a substantial risk that the property is stolen.

12.13.1 Punishment on conviction

Handling stolen property is tried on indictment and carries a maximum prison sentence of 10 years and/or an unlimited fine. The penalty imposed will not exceed that which applies to the principal offence.

12.14 POSSESSION OF STOLEN PROPERTY

Section 18 creates the offence of possession of stolen property. The offence is committed where a person without lawful authority or excuse, possesses stolen property, knowing that the property has been stolen, or reckless as to whether it has been stolen.

The *actus reus* is being in possession of stolen property.

The *mens rea* is knowledge or recklessness as to whether the property is stolen.

Section 18(2) provides that where a person has in his possession stolen property in such circumstances that it is reasonable to conclude that the person knew the property to be stolen or was reckless as to the fact, it will be presumed that the person possessing such property knew it was stolen. This presumption will be rebutted where there is a reasonable doubt as regards such knowledge or recklessness on the part of the person who has possession of the property.

12.14.1 Punishment on conviction

Possession of stolen property is tried on indictment and carries maximum prison sentence of five years and/or an unlimited fine. The penalty imposed will not exceed that which applies to the principal offence.

13. PUBLIC ORDER OFFENCES

13.1 THE CRIMINAL JUSTICE (PUBLIC ORDER) ACT 1994

Offences against public order are primarily governed by the Criminal Justice (Public Order) Act 1994. This Act repealed and updated most of the common law offences against public order. This chapter looks at the main offences covered by the Act.

13.2 INTOXICATION IN A PUBLIC PLACE

Section 4 of the Act makes it an offence for a person to be in a public place while intoxicated, to such an extent as would give rise to a reasonable apprehension that he might endanger himself or some other person.

The *actus reus* of this offence is being intoxicated in a public place. The term "intoxicated" is defined in the Act as meaning under the intoxicating influence of any substance and a "public place" is defined as including any highway, any outdoor place to which members of the public have access, a cemetery or churchyard, premises to which the public have access or a right of access on payment or otherwise, or any train, vessel or vehicle used as public transport.

The issue of *mens rea* does not really arise with this offence since it is committed by being in a public place whilst intoxicated to the extent that might give rise to the reasonable belief that a danger is posed to the defendant himself or to anyone else present.

Section 4(3) provides that if a Garda suspects, with reasonable cause, that an offence under ss.4, 5 or 6 is being committed, the Garda may seize without warrant any bottle or container and its contents which is in the possession of the accused and which the Garda has reasonable cause to suspect contains an intoxicating substance.

13.2.1 Punishment on conviction

An offence under s.4 of the 1994 Act is a summary offence and the maximum penalty is a fine of €127 (£100).

13.3 DISORDERLY CONDUCT IN A PUBLIC PLACE

Section 5 of the Act provides that it is an offence to engage in offensive conduct in a public place between the hours of 12.00 a.m. and 7.00 a.m. or at any other time after a Garda requests that the behaviour in question ceases.

The *actus reus* is engaging in offensive conduct in a public place between the relevant hours or at any time after a Garda has asked that the conduct ceases.

The *mens rea* is intention or objective recklessness.

13.3.1 Offensive conduct

Section 3 states that offensive conduct is any unreasonable behaviour which, having regard to all the circumstances, is likely to cause serious offence or annoyance to any person who is aware of such behaviour or who might reasonably be expected to be aware of it.

The purpose of s.5 is to outlaw behaviour that impacts adversely on the quality of life of others. The section is vaguely worded and it appears to create an offence of strict liability between the hours of 12.00 a.m. and 7.00 a.m. whereas the same conduct will not attract criminal liability at any other time unless the accused has refused to desist, having been requested to do so by a Garda.

13.3.2 Punishment on conviction

An offence under s.5 of the 1994 Act is a summary offence and the maximum penalty is a fine of €634.86 (£500).

13.4 THREATENING, ABUSIVE OR INSULTING BEHAVIOUR

Section 6 of the Act provides that an offence is committed by a person who uses threatening, abusive or insulting words or behaviour in a public place, with intent to provoke a breach of the peace or being reckless as to whether a breach of the peace may be occasioned.

The *actus reus* is being in a public place and using threatening, abusive or insulting words or behaving in a threatening, abusive or insulting manner.

The *mens rea* is intention or objective recklessness as regards the conduct in question and also as to whether a breach of the peace will occur.

13.4.1 Breach of the peace

A breach of the peace may occur where harm is caused to the person or property of an individual, or is likely to be caused or where an individual is put in fear of suffering harm through violence or some form of public disturbance.

13.4.2 Punishment on conviction

This is also a summary offence which carries a maximum prison sentence of three months and/or a fine of €634.86 (£500).

13.5 OBSCENE DISPLAYS

Section 7(1) makes it an offence to distribute or display in public, any writing, sign or visible representation which is threatening, abusive, insulting or obscene with intent to provoke a breach of the peace or being reckless as to whether a breach of the peace may occur.

The *actus reus* is the distribution or display, in public of anything that is threatening, abusive, insulting or obscene.

The *mens rea* is intention or objective recklessness as regards to the display or distribution of the material in question coupled with intention or objective recklessness as to whether a breach of the peace may be occasioned.

13.5.1 Obscenity

The test used to determine whether something is obscene is whether the material in question tends to deprave and corrupt those whose minds are open to such immoral influences and into whose hands such a publication may fall. As a basis for imposing criminal liability however, this is a test that could lead to arbitrariness, since what may be considered obscene by one person may well be regarded as an acceptable means of invoking the constitutionally protected right of Freedom of Expression by another.

13.5.2 Punishment on conviction

An offence under s.7 is tried summarily and carries a maximum penalty of three months' imprisonment and/or a fine of €634.86 (£500).

13.6 WILFUL OBSTRUCTION

It is an offence under s.9 of the Act to wilfully prevent or interrupt the free movement of any person or vehicle, in a public place without lawful excuse.

The *actus reus* is the prevention or interruption of the free movement of any person or vehicle in a public place, without lawful authority.

The *mens rea* is intention or wilfulness.

13.6.1 Punishment on conviction

This is a summary offence punishable by a fine not exceeding €253.95 (£200).

13.7 ENFORCEMENT OF THE ACT

Section 8 of the Act grants powers of enforcement to the Gardaí who may give an offender a direction either to desist from the conduct in question or to immediately leave the vicinity in a peaceable and orderly manner. In order to invoke s.8, the Garda must have formed the reasonable belief that an offence under ss.4, 5, 6, 7, or 9 has been committed or that the offender is loitering in a public place in circumstances which give rise to a reasonable apprehension that the safety of other people or property is under threat or that public peace may be disturbed. If the offender refuses or fails to comply with the direction of the Garda under s.8, without lawful excuse for so doing, an offence is thereby committed.

13.7.1 Punishment on conviction

An offence under s.8 is tried summarily and carries a maximum penalty of six months' imprisonment and/or a fine of €634.86 (£500).

13.8 RIOT

Section 14 of the 1994 Act abolishes the common law offence of riot and creates a new statutory offence of the same name. Riot is the most serious form of public disturbance and occurs where 12 or more persons who are present together in any place, public or private, use or threaten to use unlawful violence for a common purpose and where the conduct of those persons, taken together, is such as would cause a person of reasonable firmness, whether present or not, to fear for his safety or for that of another person. Where this occurs, each of the group who uses violence shall be guilty of riot.

Section 14(2) provides that it is immaterial whether the group of 12 or more persons use or threaten to use unlawful violence simultaneously at any place. The section further provides that the common purpose of the group may be inferred from their conduct and that it is not necessary that a person of reasonable firmness actually be present or be likely to be present. The effect or likely effect of the conduct of the group on this hypothetical person of reasonable firmness is sometimes referred to as "the notional bystander test". It should be noted that there a common purpose is not the same as a conspiracy, which is an agreement to carry out an unlawful act. No prior agreement is necessary to establish a common purpose.

The *actus reus* of riot is the use or threat of use of unlawful violence, in any place, for a common purpose by a group of 12 or more people, present together, and the actual use of violence by the defendant and the imagined reaction of a reasonable person.

The *mens rea* is intention or objective recklessness.

13.8.1 Punishment on conviction

Riot is an indictable offence which carries a maximum sentence of 10 years' imprisonment and/or an unlimited fine.

13.9 VIOLENT DISORDER

Section 15 of the 1994 Act creates the new offence of violent disorder. Section 15(5) states that references to the common law offence(s) of riot and to tumult in previous enactments are to be construed as meaning violent disorder. Section 15(6) of the 1994 Act abolishes the common law offences of rout and unlawful assembly.

Essentially, the offence of violent disorder is a lesser species of riot and may be charged as an alternative offence. Section 15(1) provides that where three or more persons present together in any place, public or private, use or threaten to use unlawful violence and the conduct of the group of three or more when taken together would cause a person of reasonable firmness to fear for his safety or that of another person, then each of the group using or threatening to use unlawful violence will be guilty of violent disorder.

The *actus reus* of violent disorder is the use or threat of use of unlawful violence, in any place, by a group of three or more people, present together, and the imagined reaction of a reasonable person.

The *mens rea* is intention or subjective recklessness. This can be seen from the wording of s.15(3) which provides that "a person shall not be convicted of the offence of violent disorder unless that person intends to use or threaten to use violence or is aware that his conduct may be violent or threaten violence".

13.9.1 Punishment on conviction

Violent disorder is tried on indictment and carries a maximum term of imprisonment of 10 years and/or an unlimited fine.

13.10 Affray

The common law offence of affray is abolished by s.16 of the 1994 Act which creates a new statutory offence of the same name. This offence in effect criminalises public brawling. Section 16(1) provides that where two or more persons use or threaten to use unlawful violence against each other in a place that is public or private or both, and that their conduct, taken together, is such that a reasonable person would be caused to fear for his safety or for that of another person, each of the group will be guilty of affray.

The *actus reus* of affray is the use or threat of use of unlawful violence towards the other person(s) present in a place which is public, private or both, and the reaction of a person of reasonable firmness to the conduct of the group, taken as a whole.

The *mens rea* is intention or subjective recklessness. Section 16(3) provides that "a person shall not be convicted of the offence of affray unless that person intends to use or threaten to use violence or is aware that his conduct may be violent or threaten violence".

For the purpose of affray, the threat of violence by words alone will not suffice; there must be some physical manifestation of the threat. It appears from the wording of the section that liability is imposed on each member of the group even where unlawful violence is only used or threatened by one person. This problem was discussed by the Court of Criminal Appeal in *People (DPP) v Reid and Kirwan* [2004] 1 I.R. 392, where Hardiman J. stated that "if that is the correct construction of the section, then, obviously, it raises questions of a far reaching nature".

13.10.1 Punishment on conviction

The offence of affray may be tried summarily or on indictment. On summary conviction the maximum penalty is a term of imprisonment of 12 months and/or a fine of €634.86 (£500); on conviction on indictment the maximum penalty is a term of imprisonment of five years and/or an unlimited fine.

13.11 Assault with Intent

Section 18 of the 1994 Act contains the offence of assault with intent to cause bodily harm or intent to commit an indictable offence. Given that the offence of common law assault has been abolished by the Non-Fatal Offences Against the Person Act 1997 and that the 1994 Act does not provide a definition for assault for the purposes of s.18, it must be supposed that an assault under s.18 is the same as an assault under s.2 of the Non-Fatal Offences Against the Person Act 1997, since the latter Act does not appear to have repealed the assault offences contained in the 1994 Act.

The *actus reus* is assault to commit bodily harm or to commit an arrestable offence.

The *mens rea* is the intention to commit the assault and the intention to commit bodily harm or an arrestable offence. It appears that recklessness would not suffice for this offence.

13.11.1 Punishment on conviction

On summary conviction the maximum penalty is 12 months' imprisonment and/or a fine of €1,269.74 (£1,000) and on conviction on indictment the maximum penalty is a term of imprisonment of five years and/or an unlimited fine.

13.12 Assault or Obstruction of a Garda

Section 38 of the Offences against the Person Act 1861 is repealed by s.19 of the Criminal Justice (Public Order) Act 1994, which creates a number of offences relating to obstruction of and assaults on a Peace Officer. For the purposes of the section, a Peace Officer is a member of the Garda Síochána, a member of the Defence Forces or a prison officer. The section also provides that an offence is committed where an assault is carried out against any person assisting a Peace Officer or where such person is obstructed whilst assisting a Peace Officer.

Section 19(1) provides that any person who:

(a) assaults a peace officer acting in the execution of the peace officer's duty, knowing that he is, or being reckless as to whether he is, a peace officer acting in the execution of his duty, or
(b) assaults any other person acting in the aid of a peace officer, or
(c) assaults any other person with intent to resist or prevent the lawful apprehension or detention of himself or any other person for any offence, is guilty of an offence.

The *actus reus* for s.19(1)(a) is an assault on a Peace Officer acting in the execution of his duty.

The *mens rea* is intention or subjective recklessness as outlined in *People (DPP) v Murray* [1977] I.R. 360.

The *actus reus* for s.19(1)(b) is assault on a person assisting a Peace Officer. The provision does not state that in this instance the Peace Officer must be acting "in the execution of his duty" but is more than likely intended to mean this.

The *mens rea* for assault is intention or recklessness. The wording of the subsection is unclear as to the *mens rea* required for the rest of the *actus reus*. It would also seem that following *People (DPP) v Murray*, the accused must have some knowledge as to the fact that the victim is assisting a Peace Officer or be subjectively reckless in this regard and that the Peace Officer is acting, as *per* s.19(1)(a) "in the execution of his duty".

The *actus reus* of s.19(1)(c) is assault in order to prevent lawful apprehension or detention of the defendant or any other person.

The *mens rea* is intention or recklessness with regard to the assault. Additionally, there must be intention as regards the resistance to, or prevention of, lawful apprehension or detention. This appears to require knowledge on the part of the defendant as regards the lawful apprehension or detention, which it appears, does not necessarily have to be effected by a Peace Officer.

13.12.1 Punishment on conviction

This offence may be tried summarily at the election of the defendant and in that instance carries a maximum penalty of 12 months' imprisonment and/or a fine of €1,269.74 (£1,000). If tried on indictment, the maximum penalty is a term of imprisonment of five years and/or an unlimited fine.

Section 19(3) provides that any person who resists or wilfully obstructs a Peace Officer in the execution of his duty or a person assisting a Peace Officer in the execution of his duty, knowing or being reckless to whether he is a Peace Officer in the execution of his duty, will have committed an offence by so doing.

The *actus reus* is resisting or wilfully obstructing a Peace Officer or anyone assisting a Peace Officer in the execution of his duty.

The *mens rea* is intention or subjective recklessness.

It might be argued that the vagueness inherent in ss.19(1)(b) and 19(1)(c) would have been largely avoided had those sections been drafted in similar terms.

13.12.2 Punishment on conviction

On summary conviction the maximum penalty is a term of six months' imprisonment and/or a fine of €634.86 (£500).

14. OFFENCES AGAINST THE STATE

There are numerous pieces of legislation that deal with conduct which is deemed to be detrimental to the interests of the State, the gravest of which is treason. For the most part, offences of this nature are contained in the Offences Against the State Act 1939 and the various amendments thereto. Other offences are located in the Official Secrets Act 1963. This chapter deals with the most important of these statutory provisions.

14.1 Treason

Article 39 of Bunreacht na hÉireann provides that:

> "Treason shall consist only in levying war against the State or assisting any state or person or inciting or conspiring with any person to levy war against the State, or attempting in force of arms or other violent means to overturn the organs of government established in this Constitution, or taking part or being concerned in or inciting or conspiring with any person to make or to take part or be concerned in any such attempt".

Article 39 is amplified by the provisions of the Treason Act 1939. Prior to the passing of the Criminal Justice Act 1990, the penalty for treason was death. Section 2 of the Criminal Justice Act now provides that treason is an offence punishable by imprisonment for life. Section 4 of the 1990 Act provides that a minimum of 40 years be served, provided the accused is an adult.

14.2 Sedition

Article 40.6.1 of Bunreacht na hÉireann grants protection to numerous rights, among which is Freedom of Expression. The Article also provides that this right may be subject to limitation on various grounds, among which are the protection of public order and the authority of the State. The Article goes on to declare that the publication or the utterance of seditious matter is an offence which shall be punishable by law. Sedition may be described as being conduct which goes beyond mere criticism of government and which is aimed at undermining the authority of the State but falls short of treason. Sedition therefore can be seen as a lesser species of treason.

Section 10(1)(c) of the Offences Against the State Act 1939 provides that it is an offence to set up in type, print, send by post, distribute, sell or offer for sale any document which is or contains or includes a seditious document.

14.3 THE OFFICIAL SECRETS ACT 1963

The Official Secrets Act 1963 contains three categories of offences. Part II of the Act deals with official information. Section 4 of the Act prohibits the disclosure of official information without authorisation to do so. Section 6 prohibits the retention of any official document or official information in the absence of any right or duty to do so.

Part III of the Act deals with offences that involve the communication of information where to do so would be prejudicial to the safety or preservation of the State.

Section 9 provides that a person shall not, in any manner prejudicial or contrary to the safety or preservation of the State, obtain, record, communicate or publish or have possession of any document or record of any of the following:

(i) the number, description, armament, equipment, disposition, movement or condition of any of the Defence Forces or of any of the vessels or aircraft belonging to the State;
(ii) any operations or projected operations of any of the Defence Forces or of the Garda Síochána or of any of the vessels or aircraft belonging to the State;
(iii) any measures for the defence or fortification of any place on behalf of the State;
(iv) munitions of war; or
(v) any other matter whatsoever information as to which would or might be prejudicial to the safety or preservation of the State.

It will be a defence to show that the defendant's conduct was authorised by the relevant Minister, someone acting on the Minister's behalf or as pursuant to his duties as a holder of public office.

Section 10 of the Act provides that where the accused is charged with an offence under s.9 and he has been in communication with or attempted to communicate, whether inside or outside the State, with a foreign agent or a member of an unlawful organisation, such communication will be evidence that his action was prejudicial to the interests of the State. Where the accused has visited the address of the foreign agent or a member of an unlawful organisation or has consorted or associated with such individuals or where the address of such individuals is found in the possession of the accused, this will constitute evidence of communication between the accused and the foreign agent or member of an unlawful organisation. The onus of proof then shifts to the accused who must prove to the contrary. The provision further defines a "foreign agent" and a "member of an unlawful organisation" and includes people who are reasonably suspected to be such.

Section 13 of the Act declares that a person who contravenes or attempts to contravene any of the provisions of the Act is liable on summary conviction to a maximum sentence of six months and/or a fine of €127 (£100). Offences under s.9 and those contained in Pt II of the Act may be tried on indictment whereupon conviction, the maximum penalty is a term of imprisonment of seven years.

14.4 THE OFFENCES AGAINST THE STATE ACTS 1939–1998

The Offences Against the State Act 1939 is the principal piece of legislation dealing with offences against the State. The purpose of the Act, as originally enacted, was to suppress activity deemed to be subversive in nature and to this end, contains some fairly radical, if not utterly draconian measures. The Act is divided into five parts with only the first three being intended to be permanent. Part V of the Act provides for the establishment of the Special Criminal Court, the jurisdiction of which has already been discussed. Section 30 of the Act deals with the arrest and detention of suspected persons and is one of only three statutory measures that allows for detention for the purposes of questioning. The constitutionality of s.30 was upheld by the Supreme Court in *People (DPP) v Quilligan* [1987] I.L.R.M. 606. Although there are 59 sections in the Act in total, relatively few of these are used with any great frequency. These are as follows:

14.4.1 Section 18

Section 18 of the 1939 Act provides that:

> "In order to regulate and control in the public interest the exercise of the constitutional right of citizens to form associations, it is hereby declared that any organisation which—
> (a) engages in, promotes, encourages, or advocates the commission of treason or any activity of a treasonable nature, or

(b) advocates, encourages, or attempts the procuring by force, violence, or other unconstitutional means of an alteration of the Constitution, or
(c) raises or maintains or attempts to raise or maintain a military or armed force in contravention of the Constitution or without constitutional authority, or
(d) engages in, promotes, encourages, or advocates the commission of any criminal offence or the obstruction of or interference with the administration of justice or the enforcement of the law, or
(e) engages in, promotes, encourages, or advocates the attainment of any particular object, lawful or unlawful, by violent, criminal, or other unlawful means, or
(f) promotes, encourages, or advocates the non-payment of moneys payable to the Central Fund or any other public fund or the non-payment of local taxation, shall be an unlawful organisation within the meaning and for the purposes of this Act, and this Act shall apply and have effect in relation to such organisation accordingly."

14.4.2 Section 19

The Government is not required to issue a declaration to the effect that a particular organisation is an unlawful one for the purposes of the Act. However, s.19 provides that the Government may make a Suppression Order with regard to any organisation where it is of the opinion that the organisation in question is an unlawful one. The Suppression Order is conclusive evidence that the organisation named within it is an unlawful organisation.

14.4.3 Section 20

A member of the organisation in respect of which the Suppression Order is made, may under s.20 of the Act, apply to either the High Court or the Attorney General for what is referred to in the Act as a "declaration of legality". This application must be made within 30 days of the making of the Suppression Order and an appeal from the decision lies to the Supreme Court. If the declaration of legality is granted, the Suppression Order "shall forthwith become null and void". No action carried out pursuant to the Suppression Order prior to the granting of the declaration of legality will be affected by this. If the declaration is not granted, and an appeal against this decision to the Supreme Court is not successful, neither the fact that the application was made nor any admissions or statements made by the applicant, whether orally or on Affidavit, in the course of the application, may be used in evidence for the purposes of any subsequent prosecution of the applicant on charges of membership of the unlawful organisation.

14.4.4 Section 52

Section 52 of the Act provides that where a suspect is detained pursuant to s.30 of the Act, the Gardaí may demand that he gives a full account of his movements and actions within a specified period and all information in his possession regarding the commission or intended commission of any offence under the Act, or any Scheduled offence, by another person. Failure or refusal to give such an account or information as demanded is an offence under s.52(2) of the Act, which offence carries a maximum penalty of six months' imprisonment. This provision has also been challenged on the grounds that it infringes the right to silence, a right protected by Bunreacht na hÉireann as being part and parcel of the right under Art.38 to a trial "in due course of law". In *Heaney v Ireland* [1996] 1 I.R. 580, the Supreme Court upheld the section on the basis that curtailment of the right to silence was a proportionate means of achieving the objective of the Offences Against the State Act 1939.

14.4.5 The Offences Against the State (Amendment) Act 1972

The 1939 Act has been amended on a number of occasions and one noteworthy example of such an amendment is to be found in s.3 of the 1972 Act.

14.4.6 Section 3

Section 3 of the Offences Against the State (Amendment) Act 1972 provides that any statements made orally or in writing or otherwise, or by any conduct by the accused which imply or lead to the reasonable inference that he is a member of an unlawful organisation, shall be evidence of such membership. "Conduct" is inclusive of a failure on the part of the accused to deny published reports of such membership. The section provides that such failure to deny published reports of membership shall not on its own be conclusive evidence of membership. Section 3(2) of the 1972 Act further provides that where a member of the Garda

Síochána, not below the rank of Chief Superintendent, states in evidence that he is of the belief that the accused is a member of an unlawful organisation, that statement shall be evidence of such membership. Section 3(2) was challenged in *O'Leary v Attorney General* [1993] 1 I.R. 102, on the grounds that it was an infringement of the presumption of innocence. The accused was found in possession of Republican posters and was convicted of membership of an unlawful organisation, the posters being deemed to have been "incriminating documents". The challenge failed on the basis that if the court agreed that the evidence did not establish the accused's guilt beyond reasonable doubt, he was entitled to be acquitted of the charge. In *People (DPP) v Ferguson* (unreported, Court of Criminal Appeal, October 27, 1975) the Court of Criminal Appeal held that the statement of the Chief Superintendent as to his belief regarding the defendant's membership of an unlawful organisation was not conclusive in and of itself as regards the charge against the accused. O'Higgins C.J. stated that where the accused denied the charge on oath "the value and cogency to be attached the expression of belief ... would be obviously very much diminished." In *People (DPP) v Mulligan* (unreported, Court of Criminal Appeal, May 17, 2004) Keane C.J. stated that "the weight to be given to that evidence [the belief of the Chief Superintendent] was entirely a matter for the court of trial."

14.4.7 The Offences Against the State (Amendment) Act 1998

Further amendments were made to the 1939 Act with the enactment, following the Omagh Bombing, of The Offences Against the State (Amendment) Act 1998. The most significant of these are as follows:

14.4.8 Section 2

Section 2 of the 1998 Act provides that where evidence is given in the course of proceedings under s.21 of the 1939 Act that the accused failed to answer any question material to the investigation of the offence, before or after being charged, the court is entitled to draw "such inferences from the failure as appear proper". Such failure may then be treated as corroborative of any other evidence but will be sufficient in and of itself for the purposes of conviction.

14.4.9 Section 6

Section 6 of the 1998 Act creates the new offence of directing an unlawful organisation, an offence punishable by life imprisonment.

The section provides that it is an offence to direct the activities of any unlawful organisation, at any level of that organisation's structure, which is the subject of a Suppression Order pursuant to s.19 of the 1939 Act.

14.4.10 Section 10

Section 10 provides for the extension of the maximum period of detention pursuant to s.30 of the 1939 Act. Since the passing of the 1998 Act, the maximum period of detention under s.30 is 72 hours.

15. INCHOATE OFFENCES

This category of offences covers attempts, conspiracy and incitement. Although sometimes referred to as incomplete offences, inchoate offences are complete offences in themselves. All that is meant by the term "incomplete" in this context is that the substantive offence that was the subject of the attempt, conspiracy or incitement may not have been carried out. This in no way reduces liability in respect of the inchoate offences.

15.1 ATTEMPT

The *actus reus* of an attempt is some conduct on the part of the accused which is sufficiently proximate to the intended offence to incur liability. If the conduct of the accused is too remote or is merely preparatory in nature, the accused will not be convicted. In *R v Eagleton* (1855) 169 E.R. 66, the accused was convicted of obtaining money by false pretences. The basic principles of the offence of attempt were outlined by the court and may be summarised as follows:

(i) Intention is not a sufficient basis upon which to establish the offence.
(ii) There must be some act(s) accompanying the intention.
(iii) The act(s) must be in some way immediately connected to the substantive offence.

The Court of Criminal Appeal ruled along similar lines in *People (AG) v Thornton* [1952] I.R. 91.

15.1.1 Proximity

The difficulty of ascertaining the exact point at which an act has gone beyond mere preparation and becomes sufficiently proximate to incur liability is not altogether clear, and will largely depend on the facts of each case. In *People (AG) v England* [1947] 1 Frewen 81, the Court of Criminal Appeal held that words alone could not amount to an attempt and that some positive action was required. In *People (AG) v Sullivan* [1964] I.R. 169, the accused, a midwife, was charged with attempting to obtain money by false pretences. The basis of the allegation was that she had devised a scheme whereby she would receive payments in respect of fictitious patients. An additional allowance was payable when the number of patients she treated went above 25. The accused duly submitted claim forms but it was not clear whether the fictitious patients were among the first 25. The Supreme Court held that for an act to be considered an attempt, it must be sufficiently proximate to the commission of the substantive offence and that where an act is the first in a series of similar actions, all carried out in furtherance of the commission of an offence, each action could be deemed sufficiently proximate to result in a conviction for attempt. Another approach that has been used in determining proximity is the so-called "last act theory". This approach is posited on the notion that where the accused has committed the last act before the substantive offence is committed, he is guilty of attempt. In *DPP v Stonehouse* [1977] 2 All E.R. 909, the accused was charged with and convicted of attempting to enable another to obtain money. The defendant, a former government minister, took out a number of life insurance policies and then faked his own death. He was subsequently discovered very much alive, although the insurance had not been claimed by his wife who was not part of the scam and believed the accused to be dead. The House of Lords upheld his conviction for attempting to commit the offence on the basis that he had done everything he could possibly have done to enable the offence to be committed, or in the words of Lord Diplock "the offender must have crossed the Rubicon and burnt his boats."

The *mens rea* for all attempts is intention. This is the case even where recklessness would be sufficient *mens rea* for the substantive offence. In *People (DPP) v Douglas and Hayes* [1985] I.L.R.M. 25, the court held that the defendants could be convicted of shooting with intent to commit murder—an offence under the Offences Against the Person Act 1861—where it could be shown that they had an intent to kill. If the intent to kill could not be proved, the defendants could not be convicted. The relevant section of the 1861 Act provided for a species of attempted murder. The modern law on attempted murder requires that the accused intended to kill; an intention to seriously injure will not suffice even though the substantive offence of murder can be proven where the accused intends to seriously injure the victim.

15.1.2 Impossibility

If the accused attempts to do something that is either legally or physically impossible, he cannot be convicted of attempt. Impossibility therefore, is a defence to a charge of attempt. In *Houghton v Smith* [1975] A.C. 476, it was held that the accused could not be convicted of handling stolen goods where the goods were not in fact stolen. Similarly, if something is a physical impossibility, it will not result in a conviction for attempt. If however, the accused intends to commit an offence and fails to succeed in his endeavour due to his own ineptitude, he will not be able to rely on the defence of impossibility.

It would appear that abandonment is not a defence to a charge of attempt on the basis that the offence is committed where the accused intends to commit the substantive offence and carries out acts sufficiently proximate to that offence.

15.1.3 Punishment on conviction

A person convicted of an attempt may be punished as though the substantive offence had actually been completed.

15.2 CONSPIRACY

A conspiracy occurs where two or more people enter into an agreement to commit an unlawful act, which can sometimes include civil wrongs. It is important to note that the actual offence need never be committed. The essence of the offence is the concluded agreement between the parties to commit an offence.

The *actus reus* of conspiracy is the agreement concluded between the parties.

The *mens rea* is the intention to commit the substantive offence. The accused need not be aware of the precise details of the substantive offence but he must have knowledge of the nature of the intended offence. In *R v Orton* [1922] V.L.R. 469, it was held that an accused could be convicted of conspiracy even where he did not know the precise details of the offence. The court held that where the accused was aware that the activity being planned was a crime, it didn't matter that he didn't know all the details. A similar ruling was given in *R v Porter* [1980] N.I.18.

Where there are a number of individuals accused of conspiring with one another, it need not be the case that each individual knew about all the others. Where someone joins in a conspiracy already hatched by others, he will also be convicted. This can be seen in the case of *AG v Oldridge* [2000] 4 I.R. 593. In this case, the accused had agreed to participate in a fraudulent scheme which had already been put into operation by others.

15.2.1 Impossibility

If the agreement entered into relates to a specific endeavour which is impossible to achieve, no conviction will follow. In *DPP v Nock* [1978] AC 979, the defendants were charged with conspiring to produce cocaine. Unknown to the accused, the material with which he was working did not contain any cocaine and consequently he could not have produced the drug. The convictions for conspiracy were quashed by the House of Lords where it was held that where the agreement between the defendants was to achieve a specific result and where that result was an impossibility, the defendants could not be convicted. The House of Lords also pointed out that where the indictment was drafted in very specific terms, no conviction could result. Where the indictment was drafted in more general terms, the court held that a conviction could be possible.

Where a party to a conspiracy subsequently pulls out of the agreement, this may amount to a mitigating factor. It would seem that a conviction could still be forthcoming since the withdrawal from the agreement is dependent on being part of the agreement to begin with.

15.2.2 Punishment on conviction

The punishment is discretionary.

15.3 INCITEMENT

Incitement occurs where the accused persuades another person to commit an offence or where a person is induced to commit an offence as a result of duress exerted by the accused. In *R v Fitzmaurice* [1983] 1 All E.R. 189, it was held that incitement could be by a suggestion, proposal or the promise of a reward. In *RRB v Applin* [1974] 2 W.L.R. 541, the court held that incitement can also occur where the accused uses threats to induce a person to commit a crime.

The *actus reus* of incitement is persuading another person, by whatever means, to engage in the commission of an offence. In this way it is similar to solicitation. The leading Irish case on incitement is *People (AG) v Capaldi* [1949] 1 Frewen 95. The defendant enquired of a doctor whether something could "be done" for a pregnant woman. Implicit in the enquiry was the doctor's willingness to perform an abortion. The doctor was also assured that money was no object, whereupon the doctor refused and asked the defendant to leave the surgery. The accused was convicted of incitement and appealed. The

Court of Criminal Appeal held that incitement involved more than the mere expression of a desire. However, in this case, the defendant had gone further than simply articulating a desire and had offered a financial incentive. On that basis, the court upheld his conviction for incitement. The incitement must be communicated either to a specific person or to a group of people. The accused can be prosecuted for attempted incitement where the communication fails for some reason. Additionally, where a person incites another to commit an offence and that other person agrees, both can then be charged with conspiracy. Where the incitee cannot in law commit an offence due, for example, to being *doli incapax*, the accused cannot be convicted of incitement.

The *mens rea* for incitement is intention. The accused must intend that the person being incited will commit the offence. Therefore, there can be no incitement if the accused knows that the incitee lacks the legal capacity to commit the offence. In *R v Whitehouse* [1977] 3 All E.R. 737, the accused was charged with incitement to commit incest. The incitee was his 15 year old daughter. Since the offence of incest by a female could only be committed by a female above the age of 16, the accused could not be convicted of incitement.

15.3.1 Impossibility

The defence of impossibility operates in much the same way with regard to incitement as it does to the other inchoate offences and its success will depend on whether the incitement relates to a specific type of act or a more general one. Impossibility may be a defence in the former, but will not be a defence in the latter.

It should be noted that where the incitee goes further than what was actually incited, the accused will not be guilty of incitement in relation to this further offence.

15.3.2 Punishment on conviction

Punishment for incitement depends on whether the substantive offence is actually committed. Where the accused is charged with incitement of a summary offence which is committed, the punishment is governed by s.22 of the Petty Sessions (Ireland) Act 1851. In the case of indictable offences, the punishment is provided for by s.7(1) of the Criminal Law Act 1997. Where the substantive offence is not actually committed, the matter of punishment is at the judge's discretion.

15.4 STATUTE

Incitement can also be a statutory offence. The Prohibition of Incitement to Hatred Act 1989 prohibits the publication, distribution or broadcast of any material that is threatening, abusive or insulting with the intention to incite hatred against a group of people or being reckless as to whether hatred is incited.

16. INTRODUCTION TO CRIMINAL DEFENCES

In order to discharge the onus of proof, the prosecution must not only prove all the elements of the offence(s) with which the defendant is charged but also negative or disprove any and all defences and explanations that are consistent with the defendant's innocence. This is part and parcel of what was referred to as "the golden thread" in *Woolmington v DPP* [1935] A.C. 462. Criminal defences may be categorised in a number of ways. Some defences are available only to a charge of murder and are partial defences only. A partial defence is one which will result in a conviction for a lesser offence than that with which the accused is charged. In the case of Provocation and Excessive Self-defence, if successfully raised, the accused will be convicted of manslaughter, having initially been tried for murder. It is also common to categorise defences according to the rationale behind them. Some defences excuse the defendant's conduct whereas others justify it. An example of the former is insanity while provocation is the clearest example of the latter.

This section of the book deals with the defences available in Irish law to an individual facing trial for a criminal offence.

17. PROVOCATION AND EXCESSIVE SELF-DEFENCE

The defence of provocation is one of two defences that apply only to murder, the other being excessive self-defence. Both are partial defences and will never justify an acquittal. An accused who successfully pleads provocation to a charge of murder will be convicted of manslaughter. In the case of offences other than murder, provocation and excessive self-defence are relevant mitigating factors which may result in a lesser sentence but they are not defences *per se*.

17.1 PROVOCATION AT COMMON LAW

The common law has long regarded individuals who act in retaliation to the provocative conduct of others as being somewhat less culpable for their actions. No such allowance is made for those who act in a cold-blooded fashion. In *R v Duffy* [1949] 1 All E.R. 932, provocation was defined as "some act, or series of acts, done by the dead man to the accused, which would cause in any reasonable person, and actually causes in the accused a sudden loss of self-control, rendering the accused so subject to passion as to make him or her for the moment not the master of his mind."

The common law encompasses therefore, both objective and subjective elements, although the English Courts have traditionally employed an objective test. The difficulties with a solely objective test can be clearly seen in *Bedder v DPP* [1954] 2 All E.R. 801, where the House of Lords rejected the argument that the particular traits of the accused should be taken into account when deciding what the reaction of the reasonable man would have been to the provocative act. In that case, the accused was assaulted and taunted by a prostitute because he was impotent. *Bedder* was highly criticised on the basis that to ignore the particular traits of the accused and to judge him by reference to the reasonable man who did not possess the same traits was absurd. The English judiciary took a different approach in the later case of *R v Camplin* [1978] 2 All E.R. 168, and essentially held that regard should be had to those characteristics of the accused that were relevant to the case, in ascertaining whether he had acted as the reasonable man would have. The accused in *Camplin* was a 15 year old boy who had been seriously sexually assaulted by an older man who had then laughed at him. The accused retaliated by hitting the man over the head with a pan, killing him. It is not entirely clear whether *Camplin* was decided on the basis that the decision in *Bedder* was incorrectly decided or because by the time *Camplin* had come about, s.3 of the Homicide Act 1957 had introduced a subjective element to the test into English law.

17.1.1 Which characteristics are relevant?

In *Bedder*, the court rejected that the defendant's impotence was a relevant issue, clearly this would not be the position post-*Camplin* and under s.3 of the 1957 Act, in England. In *R v Newell* [1980] 71 Cr. App. Rep. 331, it was held by the Court of Appeal that for a characteristic to be relevant, it had to be something significant that set the accused apart from the general population, and that the characteristic in question had to be in some way connected to the provocation.

17.2 PROVOCATION IN IRISH LAW

The leading case on the issue of provocation in Irish law is *People (DPP) v MacEoin* [1978] I.R. 27. Before considering the *MacEoin* decision and its impact on provocation in Irish law, three observations can be made:

(1) Given that the issue of provocation was governed by the common law, a question arises as to the constitutionality of the test laid down in *MacEoin*. The common law rule regarding provocation had not been challenged under the terms of Art.50 of Bunreacht na hÉireann and despite the number of decisions following *MacEoin* which all appear to have accepted the test formulated therein, it remains arguable that *MacEoin* is of dubious constitutionality. Notwithstanding the matter of the court's entitlement to reject the common law test, the same court in *People (DPP) v Noonan* [1998] 2 I.R. 439 endorsed the subjective test.

(2) The decision in *MacEoin* and in particular, the test laid down by the Supreme Court in that case has been the primary basis for most, if not all of the appeals taken against convictions arising from directions given by trial judges on the application of the *MacEoin* test. This is (or should be) a clear indication that the *MacEoin* decision itself and the test laid down in it is confusing at best, if not unconstitutional.

(3) Given that provocation is a partial defence to a charge of murder only—with the consequence that the accused will be convicted of the lesser offence of manslaughter, thus leaving the issue of sentencing to the judge's discretion—the argument might be made that if the distinction between murder and manslaughter were to be removed, the confusion over the application of the *MacEoin* test would be resolved. The full range of sentencing options would then be available to the judge, who could still impose a life sentence in the appropriate case.

17.2.1 *People (DPP) v MacEoin* [1978] I.R. 27

The accused was charged with the murder of his flatmate with whom he had been a long-term friend. Prior to the killing, both men had consumed a significant amount of alcohol. The deceased in particular, had a tendency to become aggressive while drunk. On the night of the killing, the accused returned home drunk and went to bed. He was subsequently attacked by the deceased, himself drunk. A struggle ensued, resulting in the accused losing control and hitting the deceased repeatedly with the hammer with which the deceased had initially attacked him. He was convicted of murder and appealed on the basis that he had been provoked by the deceased. The Court of Criminal Appeal rejected the common law objective test, and stated that it was no longer part of Irish law. The test, according to the Court of Criminal Appeal, was an entirely subjective one which required the jury to decide whether or not the accused had been provoked to the point where he had lost *self-control*.

17.2.2 What is provocation post-MacEoin?

Provocation is essentially the same as it had been under the common law, indeed, the court reiterated the definition cited above with the objective part of that definition omitted.

17.2.3 Must the provocation be immediate?

The essence of the defence is a sudden and temporary loss of control on the part of the deceased. However, it appears that sudden need not necessarily be immediate, but, the greater the lapse of time between the provocative conduct and the retaliation, the more difficult it will be to sustain the defence, and may indicate revenge rather than a sudden loss of control, in which case, the defence will fail.

17.2.4 Cumulative provocation

The issue of cumulative provocation has arisen primarily in the context of killings that occur in the context of spousal abuse. The English judiciary had initially been reluctant to accept that cumulative provocation could satisfy the requirement that the accused had to suddenly lose control due to the provocative conduct of the deceased. In *R v Ahluwalia* [1993] 4 All E.R. 88 and *R v Thornton (No.2)* [1996] 2 All E.R. 1023, the defendants in each case had been victims of spousal abuse who had killed their husbands. In neither case did the accused react immediately to the provocative conduct. On appeal, the conviction in *Ahluwalia* was overturned, albeit on grounds other than the issue of cumulative provocation, and a fresh appeal was allowed in the case of *Thornton*. In Thornton's case, the court held that "battered woman's syndrome" was a relevant factor to be considered when deciding whether the accused had been provoked. The Irish courts appear to have accepted the concept of cumulative provocation and will look at the most recent episode of provocation in the overall context of a longer period of abuse. Following *MacEoin*, it would appear that where the accused is the victim of long term abuse, this will be a relevant consideration given the subjective nature of the test.

17.2.5 What amounts to provocative conduct?

The common law referred to an act or series of acts and consequently, it would appear that any act, lawful or otherwise, could amount to provocation. In *R v Doughty* [1986] Crim. L.R. 625, the Court of Appeal held that a baby's crying should have been considered by the jury where the accused had been charged with the baby's murder. The defence had argued that the accused had put a pillow over the child's head in a bid to stop the child from crying. In *MacEoin*, the court referred to "wrongful acts" which could be taken to mean that the provocative conduct had to be some unlawful act. However, if the test is that of the effect of the act on the accused, there would not appear to be any logical reason to limit these acts to those that are unlawful. In *People (DPP) v Kehoe* [1992] I.L.R.M. 481, the accused killed his former girlfriend's new partner for no apparent reason other than his presence at the house of the accused's former girlfriend. In *MacEoin*, the court also stated that words can be capable of constituting provocation.

17.2.6 Who must provoke?

At common law, the provocation must have emanated from the deceased and not from a third party. It is also the case that where the accused brings about a situation and then claims to have been provoked by the deceased, he cannot rely on the defence since the provocation was self-induced.

17.2.7 Proportionality

It was stated in *MacEoin* that "if the prosecution can prove beyond reasonable doubt that the force used was unreasonable and excessive, having regard to the provocation, the defence of provocation fails". This would appear to be a rather bizarre requirement when one considers that the essence of the defence is that of the complete loss of self-control on the part of the accused.

In *People (DPP) v Mullane* (unreported, Court of Criminal Appeal, March 11, 1997), the Court of Criminal Appeal held that the jury might have been led to believe, from the directions given by the trial judge, that the amount of force used should be evaluated objectively and that this was wrong on the basis that the MacEoin test is a subjective one. A similar situation arose in *People (DPP) v Noonan* [1998] 1 I.L.R.M. 154, where again, the jury appeared to have been directed to employ an objective test in relation to the question of proportionality. The court allowed the appeal on this basis. The subjective nature of the test in relation to the proportionality of the force used was also stated in *People (DPP) v Bambrick* [1996] 1 I.R. 265, *People (DPP) v Kelly* [2000] 2 I.R. 1 and *People (DPP) v Heaney* (unreported, Court of Criminal Appeal, January 17, 2000).

17.3 EXCESSIVE SELF-DEFENCE

Like the defence of provocation, excessive self-defence is a partial defence to murder only and, if successfully pleaded, will reduce murder to manslaughter. It may be a mitigating factor in respect of other offences, resulting in a lesser sentence, but is not a defence *per se*.

17.3.1 What amounts to excessive self-defence?

Excessive self-defence occurs where the accused uses more force than is objectively necessary, but which the accused believed was necessary. Where the accused used no more force than he honestly believed was necessary, he is entitled to be acquitted of murder. The onus is on the prosecution to prove that the accused knew he was using a disproportionate amount of force. In *People (AG) v Commane* [1975] 1 Frewen 400, the Court of Criminal Appeal upheld the conviction for murder of a defendant who used force knowing it to be excessive in the circumstances. The accused had been attacked by the deceased and had struck the deceased in self-defence. Having knocked the deceased unconscious, the accused then strangled him.

In *People (AG) v Dwyer* [1972] I.R. 416, the accused stabbed the deceased in the course of a brawl. He claimed that he did so because he believed that the deceased had a knife and was, consequently, afraid for his life. The Supreme Court held that the accused's subjective belief was sufficient to reduce the offence from murder to manslaughter.

The position in English law is different and in that jurisdiction, excessive self-defence will not reduce murder to manslaughter but may go towards mitigation of sentence. The House of Lords held in *R v Clegg* [1995] 1 All E.R. 334, that a British soldier who had shot and killed a passenger in a car which had driven through a checkpoint in Belfast, could not argue excessive self-defence when he was charged with the murder. His defence had been that he had fired four bullets at the passing car in order to defend a colleague who was standing nearby and that excessive self-defence should be accepted on that basis. Forensic evidence revealed that the fatal bullet had been fired after the car had passed the soldiers, and the defendant was convicted.

18. INTOXICATION

There is no general defence of intoxication at common law. The issue arises where an accused argues that due to intoxication, he lacked capacity to form *mens rea*. At the outset, it should be stressed that intoxication is not the same as drunkenness. Whereas the former may well have a bearing on liability, if it can be shown to have deprived the accused of the capacity to form the required intent for the offence with which he is charged, the latter will, almost invariably, be regarded as an aggravating factor with the consequent implications in respect of sentencing.

The rationale behind the defence is based on a mixture of principle and policy. It is not desirable that a person could be convicted of an offence where he could not have formed the intention to commit it. On the other hand, it is accepted that the public should be afforded some form of protection against the actions of those who become so intoxicated as to pose a threat through criminal activity. The defence of intoxication may, therefore, be viewed as a form of balancing act between these two considerations. Certain limitations are imposed on the application of the defence.

18.1 DISTINCTION BETWEEN CRIMES OF BASIC/SPECIFIC INTENT

An offence of basic intent is one which requires no more than the performance of a particular act, for example, rape or assault. An offence of specific intent is one which requires an intention to bring about a particular outcome; the clearest example of a crime of specific intent, sometimes known as a result offence, is murder.

In *DPP v Beard* [1920] All E.R. 21, the House of Lords held that while drunkenness is never a defence, intoxication could be where the defendant was rendered incapable of forming the specific intent to commit the offence in question. In this case, the accused had been charged with murder, which is an offence of specific intent. The issue was further considered in *DPP v Majewski* [1976] 2 All E.R. 142, which has come to be regarded as the leading authority on intoxication. In *Majewski*, the accused had been charged with numerous counts of assault occasioning bodily harm. Prior to the incident, the accused had consumed a considerable quantity of alcohol and drugs and then sought to rely on the fact that he could not have formed *mens rea* due to intoxication. The House of Lords reiterated the position that at common law there was no defence of intoxication but that there were some exceptions to this general rule. The main point made by the House of Lords in *Majewski* was that where an offence was one of specific intent, intoxication could be a defence if it had the effect of depriving the accused of the capacity to form *mens rea*. Offences of basic intent were held not to be covered by the defence on the basis that they could be committed recklessly, and since becoming intoxicated was, in itself, reckless, the defence could not apply.

The *Majewski* decision was criticised as being illogical on the basis that the distinction drawn between offences of specific and basic intent was artificial. The Lords themselves acknowledged that drawing a distinction between the two types of offence was illogical but that public policy considerations tipped the balance in favour of doing so. *Majewski* was not followed in all common law jurisdictions, having been rejected by the High Court of Australia in *The Queen v O'Connor* [1980] 146 CLR 64 and eventually by the Canadian Supreme Court in *R v Daviault* [1994] 3 SCR 63.

18.2 Voluntary/Involuntary Intoxication

Voluntary intoxication occurs where the accused consumes or ingests some form of intoxicant of his own volition as occurred in *Majewski*. An intoxicant may be alcohol or may be some other form of drug. In *R v Lipman* [1970] 1 QB 152, the accused had taken LSD and killed his girlfriend due to the belief that he was being attacked by snakes. This belief was caused by the hallucinogenic effects of the drug. He was convicted of manslaughter and appealed on the basis that he had no idea what he was doing and had not intended to kill the victim. The Court of Appeal upheld the conviction on the basis that manslaughter can be committed through the commission of an unlawful and dangerous act and that because it was not necessary to have specific intent, self-induced (voluntary) intoxication was not a defence.

In *R v Hardie* [1984] 3 All E.R. 848, the accused took a number of Valium tablets because he was upset about breaking up with his girlfriend. Rather than becoming calm, the accused became aggressive and ended up starting a fire in his former girlfriend's apartment. Having taken the tablets voluntarily, the question arose as to whether he could rely on the defence of intoxication. In this case, the court held that the accused could not have known that the tablets could cause aggression and therefore, could not have been voluntarily intoxicated. The accused was deemed to have been involuntarily intoxicated but the court stated that had he known that the drug could have induced aggressive behaviour, the defence would not have been available.

Involuntary intoxication arises where the accused takes an intoxicating substance unwittingly. In these cases, the accused will have the defence of intoxication available even for crimes of basic intent. In *R v Allen* [1988] Crim. L.R. 698, it was held that the defence is not available if the accused knows that the substance is an intoxicant, but is unaware of its potency.

The defence is not available in cases where intent is not actually negatived. Most, if not all intoxicating substances lower inhibitions. Consequently, where the accused has formed the intent to commit an offence, albeit because his inhibitions were reduced due to the consumption of an intoxicant, the defence will not be available on the basis that, according to the court in *R v Kingston* [1994] 3 All E.R. 353, "a drugged intent is still an intent".

18.3 DUTCH COURAGE

Intoxication will not be a defence where the accused has taken alcohol or drugs in order to give him the courage to carry out an offence. In *AG for Northern Ireland v Gallagher* [1961] 3 All E.R. 299, the accused, having formed the intention to kill his wife, consumed a considerable amount of alcohol in order to give him the courage to do so. He then argued that he had been intoxicated to such an extent that he lacked capacity to form the required intention, and that even though he had formed such an intent earlier, the *mens rea* and the *actus reus* did not coincide at the time of the killing. His conviction for murder was upheld by the House of Lords, where it was held that intoxication was not available as a defence in a case of Dutch courage and that the killing could be viewed as a continuing act, the *mens rea* still being operative at the time of the killing.

18.4 INTOXICATION IN IRISH LAW

Until recently, it was unclear whether the *Majewski* decision had any application in this jurisdiction. The issue of intoxication has not been raised very frequently before the Irish courts. In *People (AG) v Manning* [1953] 89 I.L.T.R. 155, the court stated that the effect of drink had to go much further than to lower the accused's inhibitions. It also appears that the court in *Manning* drew a distinction between crimes of specific and basic intent, and stated that in terms of a defence to murder, intoxication would only have the effect of reducing the charge to one of manslaughter. Similarly, in *People (DPP) v McBride* [1997] I.L.R.M. 233, the Court of Criminal Appeal seemed to accept the principle that intoxication could be relevant in terms of the accused's ability to form *mens rea*.

The question of whether *Majewski* is applicable in this jurisdiction has now been answered in the affirmative by the Court of Criminal Appeal in *People (DPP) v John Reilly* [2004] I.E.C.C.A.10.

In this case, the accused was charged with murder and argued that he was intoxicated to the extent that he could not have formed the *mens rea* for the offence. It was common cause that the accused remembered nothing of the incident, in which an infant was found dead beside the accused. The child had died from multiple stab wounds inflicted by a knife owned by, and in the possession of, the accused. On the night in question, the accused had been drinking heavily in his cousin's house, and had fallen asleep in the early hours of the morning in the sitting room. A cot of sorts had been made up for the baby using two armchairs. The child's mother got up the next morning and went to check on the child, only to discover that he was dead. The accused was asleep in the couch with the knife nearby. He was convicted of manslaughter and appealed. The Court of Criminal Appeal not only acknowledged the inherent illogicality of the distinction drawn between crimes of basic and specific intent in *Majewski*, but went further and stated that issues arising in the case could not be determined by pure logic. The court looked to the decision of the High Court in Australia in *The Queen v O'Connor* and to the decisions of the Canadian Supreme Court, which had initially accepted the *Majewski* ruling in *Leary v The Queen* [1977] 74 Dir (3d) 103 and in *R v Bernard* [1988] 2 SCR 833, but later overruled these in *R v Daviault*. The Court of Criminal Appeal refused to follow the rulings in *O'Connor* and *Daviault* and held instead that the ruling of the trial judge, which had been based on the *Majewski* decision, was correct. The position of intoxication in Irish law therefore is that which was laid down by the Court of Criminal Appeal in *Reilly*, which is the same as the position in England and Wales under the *Majewski* decision.

19. AUTOMATISM

The defence of automatism overlaps in certain respects with the defences of insanity and intoxication. Unlike insanity however, the defence of automatism will result in an acquittal if successfully pleaded. Insanity, as we have already seen, will, if successfully invoked, lead to the detention of the individual under the Criminal Law (Insanity) Act 2006. Another procedural distinction exists between the two defences: where the defence of automatism is raised, it will be for the prosecution to disprove it; whereas, the accused who wishes to plead insanity must prove that he was insane, albeit on the balance of probabilities.

19.1 Definition

The definition of automatism was given in *Bratty v AG for Northern Ireland* [1961] 3 All E.R. 523, where it was said to be "an act done by the muscles without any control by the mind such as a spasm, a reflex action or a convulsion, or an act done whilst suffering from a concussion or whilst sleep-walking". In its most basic form, the defence of automatism arises where the accused had no control over his body. It is the involuntary nature of the actions that gives rise to the defence. This can be clearly seen in the case of *R v Boshears* (The Times, February 8, 1961) where the accused had killed a woman while he was asleep. He was acquitted on the basis that he had no control over his actions and could not therefore be responsible for them.

19.2 Internal and External Factors

Where the automatic state is brought about by an internal factor, whether a physical or mental condition, it is viewed as being a disease of the mind and is consequently regarded as a form of insanity. This type of automatism is therefore, insane automatism. In this situation, the M'Naghten Rules apply, and if successful, will lead to a verdict of "not guilty by reason of insanity".

External factors are those that occur outside the body of the accused but which cause him to respond reflexively. In this type of situation, the defence of automatism, if accepted by the jury, will result in an acquittal on the basis that the accused had no control over his actions.

Where an external factor causes an internal factor, it is open to the jury to find that the automatism was caused by the external factor. In this situation, much depends on the facts of any given case.

In *R v T* [1990] Crim. L.R. 607, the accused had been suffering from post-traumatic stress disorder brought about by being the victim of rape. She was charged with robbery and the court held that the issue of non-insane automatism should have been left to the jury on the basis that the post-traumatic stress disorder (internal factor) had in fact been caused by the rape (external factor).

Further confusion arises where the accused is suffering from some medical condition and commits an offence whilst in a state of automatism arising from that condition. In particular, cases involving diabetics have given rise to questions about whether the automatism is due to an internal or external factor and whether the automatism could be said to be self-induced.

19.3 SELF-INDUCED AUTOMATISM

Automatism is self-induced where an accused has brought the automatic state about due to the consumption of alcohol or other intoxicant; in this situation, the matter is essentially one of intoxication. The decision of the Court of Criminal Appeal in *People (DPP) v John Reilly* is relevant to this issue on two grounds. First, the decision in *Reilly* is an acceptance by the Irish judiciary of the ruling in *DPP v Majewski* [1976] 2 All E.R. 142, and secondly, the defence of automatism was raised in *Reilly*. The accused had consumed a substantial quantity of alcohol and fell asleep. At some point during the night, a baby, sleeping on a nearby chair was stabbed repeatedly and killed by the accused, who had no recollection of the incident. A key element of the defence's argument was that even though the accused had fallen into a deep sleep due to the consumption of alcohol, the cause of the automatism was the deep sleep and not the intoxication. It was argued that this ought to have been put to the jury and that if the jury accepted this proposition, an acquittal should have followed. In clarifying the issue for the jury the trial judge stated that "you have heard a lot of expert evidence in relation to things happening during sleep and if you do something that you have no control over, say the epileptic or the diabetic in a hypo or a hyper as the case may be, if they do something that they absolutely have no control over then they do not have criminal liability for that. You must do something by having a free choice, even a drunken free choice, to have criminal liability for it. ... I left it open to you that if you find a free standing situation in which the accused had no control over his actions, then he would not be criminally liable and he would be entitled to a verdict of not guilty. But if that situation has come about because of his voluntary consumption of alcohol then you look instead to the law of intoxication."

The jury went on to convict the accused of manslaughter and the key issue for the appeal court was whether the trial judge's direction to the jury was a correct statement of the law. The Court of Criminal Appeal held that the trial judge's direction had been correct and that where the accused, at the time of the killing, had no control over himself and that his lack of control had been caused by his voluntary consumption of alcohol, the matter was to be decided on the basis of *Majewski*.

The older cases concerning diabetics are relevant to this issue also. In *R v Quick* [1973] 3 All E.R. 347, a diabetic had taken insulin, had then not eaten properly and had consumed too much alcohol, causing him to suffer from hypoglycaemia. Whilst in this condition he assaulted the victim. His defence argued that he had been in a state of automatism. The trial judge stated that insanity was more appropriate. On this basis, the accused entered a plea of guilty and subsequently appealed his conviction. It was held on appeal that his condition had been brought about due to taking insulin (an external factor) and not due to the diabetes (an internal factor). This being the case, the court held that the jury should have been given the opportunity to consider the defence of automatism. The court also held that automatism would not be a defence where the accused consumed drink or drugs or where he had done or omitted to do something, the result of which could reasonably be foreseen. In *R v Bailey* [1983] 2 All E.R. 503, facts similar to those in *Quick* were considered by the court, the main difference here being that the accused was charged with an offence of specific, rather than basic intent. The defence argued that he lacked capacity, due to automatism, to form the necessary intent and that the defence of automatism applied even where it was self-induced. In *Bailey*, the court held that the decision in *Quick* as regards the application of the defence with regard to offences of basic intent was correct and that in such cases self-induced automatism was no defence. The court drew a distinction between situations in which the consumption of alcohol or drugs brought about an automatic state and those in which the automatic state was brought about inadvertently; the defence being unavailable for the former and available for the latter. Crucial to this matter was the foresight of the accused. The court held that the effects of insulin coupled with the effects of not eating properly might not be known to the accused and that knowledge of these could not be assured. Where the accused knew what might happen and had gone on to take a risk, he would have been reckless and could then be convicted of an offence of basic intent. Where this was not the case, and even where the accused didn't eat properly after taking insulin, he would have a valid defence. The difference between the two cases appears to be that one related to an offence of basic intent and self-induced automatism was held not to be a defence (*Bailey*) whereas the other involved an offence of specific intent and the issue of liability was deemed to rest on the foresight of the accused. Where the accused could have foreseen the effects of taking insulin and not eating properly, he could not rely on the defence of automatism. If, however, the accused could not have foreseen the effects, the defence could apply.

20. INSANITY

The law on insanity has recently been given a radical overhaul with the implementation of the Criminal Law (Insanity) Act 2006 which came into effect on June 1, 2006. The 2006 Act repeals most of the old legislation governing insanity with the Criminal Lunatics Act 1800 and the Trial of Lunatics Act 1883 being repealed in their entirety. Prior to the enactment of the new legislation, the law on insanity was of relevance in two ways in the context of the criminal law. The first of these was with regard to the fitness of the accused person to stand trial and the second related to the application of the insanity defence itself. As a defence, insanity is of general application in Irish law and was, until the passing of the new Act, an "all or nothing defence".

20.1 THE CRIMINAL LAW (INSANITY) ACT 2006

20.1.1 Section 4—Fitness to be tried

An accused cannot be tried if he is not fit to plead—to do so would be in flagrant breach of the rights of the accused to have a fair trial. Prior to the enactment of the 2006 Act, the term "fitness to plead" was used; this term has now been replaced with "fitness to be tried". Section 4(2) provides that "an accused person shall be deemed unfit to be tried if he or she is unable by reason of mental disorder to understand the nature and course of the proceedings". The term "mental disorder" is defined in s.1 as including "mental illness, mental disability, dementia or any disease of the mind but does not include intoxication". If, by reason of mental disorder, the accused is unable to:

(a) plead to the charge;
(b) instruct counsel;
(c) elect for jury trial where the offence with which he is charged is an "either-or" offence;
(d) make a proper defence;
(e) in the case of a jury trial, challenge a juror to whom he may wish to object; or
(f) understand the evidence,
the accused will be deemed unfit to be tried.

The criteria laid down in s.4 regarding the test of the accused's fitness to plead are based on those laid down by the courts, particularly those outlined by the Supreme Court in *State (Coughlan) v Minister for Justice* [1968] I.L.T.R.177, where it was held that the question to be answered is whether the accused person has "sufficient intellect to comprehend the course of the proceedings of the trial, so as to make a proper defence, to challenge a juror to whom he may wish to object, and to understand the details of the evidence". Section 4 therefore mirrors the decision in *Coughlan* very closely.

Where the accused is deemed unfit to be tried summarily, in accordance with s.4(3), the court may, if it is satisfied on the evidence of an approved medical officer, commit the accused to a specified designated centre for care or treatment on an in-patient or out-patient basis, as appropriate. Similar provisions apply in the case of an accused charged with an indictable offence. The proceedings will then be adjourned until further order of the court.

The issue of fitness to plead relates to the mental capacity of the accused at the time of the trial—not at the time of the commission of the alleged offence.

20.1.2 Section 5—Verdict

Prior to the passing of the 2006 Act, the verdict in the case of an accused person who successfully invoked the insanity defence was "guilty but insane". The verdict sounded contradictory due to the use of the word "guilty" although it was held in *People (DPP) v Gallagher* [1991] I.L.R.M. 339 to be in fact, an acquittal. Section 5 provides that where, at the time of the commission of the alleged offence the accused was:

(a) suffering from a mental disorder, and
(b) the mental disorder was such that the accused person shouldn't be held responsible because he didn't know the nature and quality of the act or did not know that what he was doing was wrong or was unable to refrain from committing the act,

the court shall return a special verdict to the effect that the accused is "not guilty by reason of insanity". Section 5 therefore incorporates aspects of the M'Naghten rules, which will be dealt with below, and also the concept of irresistible impulse.

20.1.3 Section 6(1)—Diminished responsibility

Where the charge against the accused is one of murder and the court finds that the accused carried out the alleged killing and was at the time of the killing, suffering from a mental disorder which would not justify a finding of not guilty by reason of insanity, but did diminish substantially the accused's responsibility, the court will find the accused not guilty of murder, but guilty of manslaughter. Section 6(3) provides that a woman found guilty of infanticide may be dealt with under s.6(1). Even before the passing of the 2006 Act, it is likely, following the decision in *Doyle v Wicklow County Council* [1974] I.R. 55, that an accused could rely on the defence of insanity in situations where his ability to exercise judgment was in some way diminished.

20.1.4 Appeals

Sections 7 and 8 provide for appeals against findings of unfitness to be tried and against the "not guilty by reason of insanity" verdict respectively. There were no such provisions under the repealed legislation.

20.2 THE MENTAL HEALTH (CRIMINAL LAW) REVIEW BOARD

In keeping with the obligations of the European Convention on Human Rights, s.11 provides for the establishment of An Bord Athbhreithnithe Meabhair-Shláinte (An Dlí Coiriúl)/The Mental Health (Criminal Law) Review Board. The Board will be an independent body with responsibilities and powers conferred on it under the 2006 Act. Those powers are set out in s.12 which include the regular review of the detention of individuals detained following the passing of the special verdict or those who are detained in designated centres following a finding of unfitness to be tried. The Review Board, in carrying out its functions, may, among other things, direct in writing the consultant psychiatrist responsible for the care and treatment of a patient whose case is being reviewed by the Board, to arrange for the patient to attend before the Board, or direct in writing any person whose evidence is required by the Board to attend before the Board to provide such evidence. Failure to comply with the directions of the Board and, further, anything done in relation to the proceedings before the Board which, if done in relation to proceedings before a court by a witness, would amount to contempt of court is an offence punishable on summary conviction by a maximum term of 12 months' imprisonment and/or a fine of €3,000.

20.3 THE DEFENCE OF INSANITY

Where the accused, having been deemed fit to stand trial, wishes to raise the defence of insanity, the burden of proof shifts to him and this burden may be discharged on the civil standard of proof (*i.e.* on the balance of probabilities). The burden then shifts back to the prosecution who must disprove the defence beyond a reasonable doubt. The defence as it is known today emerged in *R v Hadfield* (1800) 27 St. Tr. 1281. The defendant believed that he had to kill himself in order to save mankind but, believing suicide to be a sin, he elected to shoot the King instead in the hope that he would be hanged. He was charged with treason, which was a capital offence. The court held that he was insane and he was duly acquitted. The rules governing the issue of insanity were formulated by the Law Lords following the acquittal on grounds of insanity of the accused in *R v M'Naghten* [1843] All E.R. 229. The accused, while suffering from a delusion that he was being persecuted by the Tory Party, decided to shoot Sir Robert Peel, but shot and killed Peel's Secretary instead. He was acquitted on the basis that he was insane. The subsequent public outcry prompted the House of Lords to pose a number of questions regarding the matter to the Law Lords. The responses to those questions are known as the M'Naghten Rules and are the exclusive test of insanity in English Law. In *R v Windle* [1952] 2 All E.R. 1, the accused was convicted of the murder of his wife, believing, due to mental illness, that it was morally right to do so. The accused did, however, know that his conduct was legally wrong. He sought to rely on the defence of insanity, but was precluded from doing so because he knew that he had been acting unlawfully and consequently, could not avail of the M'Naghten Rules. The court held that as far as the law in England is concerned, the defence of insanity is based entirely on the M'Naghten Rules. In Ireland, the M'Naghten Rules are the primary test but are not the "sole and exclusive test". This was held by the Supreme Court in *People (AG) v O'Brien* [1936] I.R. 236 and was upheld in *Doyle v Wicklow County Council* [1974] I.R. 55.

20.4 THE M'NAGHTEN RULES

Any discussion of the application of the M'Naghten Rules from the point of view of Irish law must proceed on the basis that firstly, they are not the sole test for insanity in Irish criminal law, although they have been the primary test, and secondly, must now be construed in light of the provisions of the 2006 Act.

(1) Where the accused is suffering from a partial delusion but knows, despite the delusion, that his actions are unlawful, he will have no defence.
(2) Every person is presumed to be sane but this presumption is rebuttable.
(3) The accused must show that when he committed the offence, he was suffering from a defect of reason caused by a disease of the mind, and that he didn't know the nature and quality of his actions, that he did not know they were unlawful.
(4) An accused person suffering from a partial delusion should be treated as though the facts of his delusion were real.

20.4.1 Defect of reason from a disease of the mind

Defect of reason from a disease of the mind in this context can include conditions arising from other medical conditions. In *R v Kemp* [1957] 1 QB 399, the accused attacked his wife with a hammer. He was found to have been suffering from a defect of reason from a disease of the mind brought on by arteriosclerosis, a medical condition which had caused congestion of blood in his brain. In *Ellis v DPP* [1990] 2 I.R. 291, the accused was charged with murder and sought to rely on the defence of automatism on the basis that he was suffering from the effects of epilepsy at the time of the killing. The judge directed the jury to disregard the issue of automatism and to consider the issue of insanity. The accused was found to be guilty but insane. In *R v Quick* [1973] 3 All E.R. 347, the defendant was a diabetic, who neglected to follow medical advice in relation to his condition. While suffering from hypoglycaemia as a result, he committed an assault. He argued that he should be acquitted on the basis of automatism but the trial judge directed that his defence was that of insanity. On that basis, he entered a plea of guilty and subsequently appealed his conviction. The Court of Appeal held that the defendant's condition had been brought about by his failure to follow medical advice. As this was an external factor, there was no disease of the mind and consequently the defendant could not avail of the defence of insanity. In *R v Sullivan* [1983] 2 All E.R. 673, the opposite conclusion was arrived at in the case of an epileptic who committed an assault. In this case, the court followed the decisions in *Kemp* and *Quick* and found that epilepsy, being an internal factor, gave rise to a defence of insanity. The defence is not available to someone who, through lack of care or through absent-mindedness, commits an offence. In *R v Clarke* [1972] 1 All

E.R. 219, the accused tried to assert that forgetfulness, caused by depression, had caused her to shoplift. At her trial, it was held that this could give rise to the defence but the proposition was rejected on appeal where the court held that the defence avails those who have, through a defect of reason from a disease of the mind, lost the power to reason and did not apply to those who simply failed to exercise that reason.

20.4.2 Nature and quality of the act

In addition to the foregoing, the accused must also show that he either did not know the nature and quality of the act or that if he did, that he did not know it was unlawful. The lack of knowledge regarding the nature and quality or unlawfulness of the act must have been caused by the defect in reason.

In *R v Codere* (1916) 12 Cr. App. Rep. 21, a soldier was convicted of the murder of a fellow soldier. He had argued that "nature" and "quality" suggested that there were different considerations to have regard to in the context of insanity. "Nature", he argued referred to the physical aspect of the act while "quality" referred to its moral character. The Court of Appeal held that the belief of the accused with regard to the moral aspect of the act was of no consequence. He could still be convicted if he knew he was killing someone, regardless of what his reasons for doing so might be. In *R v Dickie* [1984] 3 All E.R. 173, the accused knowingly started a fire. The fact that he was suffering from a manic-depressive condition at the time was held not to be relevant, what mattered was that he was aware of the nature and quality of his action.

20.4.3 The wrongful nature of the act

The accused must also have been aware of the wrongfulness of his actions. Wrongfulness in this context means unlawful. Where the accused knew that his actions were unlawful, the defence will fail. In *R v Windle* [1952] 2 All E.R. 1, the accused killed his wife by giving her an overdose. She had frequently asserted that she wished to commit suicide and there was evidence that she was insane. The court even accepted that the accused might have been suffering from a form of insanity communicated to him from his wife.

Despite this, the defence failed because the accused had stated to the police "I suppose they will hang me for this." This statement by the accused showed that he appreciated that his actions were unlawful notwithstanding the probability that he himself was suffering from some form of mental disorder.

20.4.4 Irresistible impulse

In English law, the issue of irresistible impulse can be viewed as a form of diminished responsibility in cases of murder only. The effect of the defence is to reduce a charge of murder to one of manslaughter. Outside of that limited situation, irresistible impulse is not covered. The M'Naghten Rules exclude the concept and this point has been made in a number of English cases. In *R v Kopsch* (1925)19 Cr. App. Rep. 50, the notion that the accused could not prevent himself from strangling his aunt was described as "a fantastic and subversive theory". The point was made in even starker terms in *R v Creighton* (1909) 14 CCC 349, where the accused was informed that "if you cannot resist an impulse in any other way, we will hang a rope in front of your eyes, and perhaps that will help."

The Irish position on the matter is different. As stated previously, the M'Naghten Rules are not the sole and exclusive test of insanity in this jurisdiction and in the context of irresistible impulse the Irish judiciary have accepted that this can be viewed as a form of insanity. This has now been put on a statutory footing in s.5 of the 2006 Act which expressly provides for the concept of irresistible impulse. In *People (AG) v Hayes* (unreported, Court of Criminal Appeal, November 30, 1967) the Court of Criminal Appeal held that in the case of an accused person who had killed his wife in circumstances where he could not stop himself from doing so, the defence of insanity should be available, notwithstanding the fact that the accused was aware of the nature and quality of his actions and knew they were wrong, but was unable to prevent himself from committing them due to a defect of reason caused by a disease of the mind. In *Doyle v Wicklow County Council* [1974] I.R. 55, the Supreme Court reiterated this position. In *People (AG) v McGrath* [1960] 1 Frewen 267, the Court of Criminal Appeal rejected the argument that a conviction ought to be overturned on the grounds that the accused was acting under an irresistible impulse. Although the appeal failed, it was not because the court wouldn't accept that irresistible impulse was a form of insanity, but rather because there was no evidence to support the claim that the accused had in fact been suffering from it. In *(AG) v Hayes* (unreported, Central Criminal Court, November 30, 1967) Henchy J. held that the defence of insanity could not be denied to an accused where, due to an irresistible impulse, caused by mental illness, the accused had killed his wife. This was upheld in *Doyle v Wicklow County Council* [1974] I.R. 55, where the Supreme Court held that it would be unjust to deny the defence of insanity in the case of an accused who, suffering from mental illness, was unable to resist the impulse to burn down an abattoir.

20.4.5 The consequences of the plea of insanity

In *People (DPP) v Gallagher* [1991] I.L.R.M. 339, the Supreme Court held that the verdict of "guilty but insane" was in fact, an acquittal. Prior to the passing of the 2006 Act, the individual found guilty but insane was detained under s.2(2) of the Trial of Lunatics Act 1883, "during the government's pleasure". The Supreme Court in *Gallagher* also stated that the issue of the release of such an individual is a matter for the Executive, but that the individual so detained could apply to be released on the grounds that he was no longer insane or a danger. The defendant in *Gallagher* sought release from detention on the grounds that he had recovered from his insanity, but was unsuccessful. He eventually absconded and left the jurisdiction. Extradition proceedings were mounted but were unsuccessful due to the fact that he had not been convicted of any offence which would have justified his extradition back to this State. He remains at large. The government or the relevant Minister would then be obliged to enquire into the continued detention, and the conclusion reached would not be reviewable by the courts. It would appear that the refusal to conduct such an enquiry might give rise to judicial review proceedings. It does seem odd that a person, who by definition was sane, having been deemed fit to stand trial could have been detained indefinitely (or at all) following the verdict under s.2(2) of the 1883 Act.

The 2006 Act makes provision for the detention of accused persons found not guilty by reason of insanity "if the court, having considered any report submitted to it ... and such other evidence as may be adduced before it, is satisfied that an accused person found not guilty by reason of insanity ... is suffering from a mental disorder (within the meaning of the Act of 2001) and is in need of in-patient care or treatment in a designated centre, the court shall commit that person to a specified designated centre until an order is made under Section 13". Section 13 of the 2006 Act deals with the review of detention. The fact that "mental disorder" is to be construed within the meaning of the Mental Health Act 2001 means that a person suffering from a condition such as diabetes is unlikely to find themselves detained following a verdict of not guilty by reason of insanity.

21. SELF-DEFENCE

The common law has always recognised the right to use a reasonable amount of force in order to defend oneself or a close relative from attack and for the purposes of preventing the commission of a criminal offence. In *People (AG) v Keatley* [1954] I.R. 12, the Court of Criminal Appeal stated that there was no need, in this jurisdiction, to show that the accused had any special relationship with the person whom he sought to protect from attack. The justifiable use of force is now provided for by ss.18 and 19 of the Non-Fatal Offences Against the Person Act 1997. A question arises as to whether the common law rules in relation to self-defence have been totally abolished or merely abolished within the meaning of ss.18 and 19.

Section 22 (1) provides that:

"The provisions of this Act have effect subject to any enactment or rule of law providing a defence, or providing lawful authority, justification or excuse for an act or omission".

Section 22 (2) provides as follows:

"Notwithstanding subsection (1) any defence available under the common law in respect of the use of force within the meaning of ss.18–19 or an act immediately preparatory to the use of force for the purposes mentioned in Sections 18–19 is hereby abolished".

21.1 Justifiable Use of Force

Section 18 provides that "the use of force by a person for any of the following purposes, if only such as is reasonable in the circumstances as he believes them to be, does not constitute an offence."

- (a) to protect himself or herself or a member of the family of that person or another from injury, assault or detention caused by a criminal act; or
- (b) to protect himself or herself or (with the authority of that other) another from trespass to the person; or
- (c) to protect his or her property from appropriation, destruction or damage caused by a criminal act or from the trespass or infringement; or

(d) to protect property belonging to another from appropriation, destruction or damage caused by a criminal act or (with the authority of that other) from trespass or infringement; or
(e) to prevent crime or a breach of the peace.

The section clearly permits the use of force to protect a third party from injury, assault or detention caused by a criminal act. In doing this, the Act gives statutory expression to the common law position. In *People (AG) v Keatley* [1954] I.R. 12, the accused had been convicted of the manslaughter of a man who had attacked the accused's brother. The conviction was appealed on the grounds that the trial judge's direction to the jury had been incorrect. The Court of Criminal Appeal held that the jury should have been told that the use of force to prevent a crime was permissible provided that the amount of force used was not excessive. The use of force to protect a third party is not permitted in some other jurisdictions unless it can be shown that there is a close relationship between the accused and the person whom he sought to protect. This can be seen in *Devlin v Armstrong* [1971] N.I. 13, where charges of incitement to riot and of breaches of public order were brought against Bernadette Devlin. Her defence argued that she had been acting in legitimate defence of herself and other residents of Derry's Bogside. The court refused to accept the defence on the grounds that there was no special relationship between the accused and those whom she had purported to defend.

Section 18(1) provides that the defendant will be able to rely on the defence of justifiable use of force if he uses reasonable force for any of the above reasons.

Section 18(5) provides that the matter of whether the defendant was operating under one of the above grounds will be determined according to the defendant's subjective view of the situation. Section 18 also provides that "crimes" and "criminal acts" include those which would be deemed criminal even where an accused could be acquitted on grounds of automatism, duress, infancy, intoxication or insanity.

At common law, a defendant who uses force in response to a mistaken belief as to the existence of a threat is entitled to be judged according to his subjective (albeit mistaken) view of the circumstances.

Section 18(7) of the Act provides that generally, a defendant will not be able to rely on the defence where he has caused or brought about a state of affairs with the intention of using force to resist its consequences. An exception to the general rule exists where the defendant is engaged in lawful conduct even where he knows that it may provoke an unlawful response from others.

Section 19(1) of the Act allows for the use of reasonable force to carry out a lawful arrest and provides that: "The use of force by a person in effecting or assisting in a lawful arrest, if only such as is reasonable in the circumstances as he or she believes them to be, does not constitute an offence". Section 19(3) provides that the lawfulness or otherwise of the arrest will be judged according to the subjective view of the defendant. This allows for the defendant to be judged according to a mistaken belief.

21.2 FORCE

Section 20 of the Act defines "force" and provides that:

> "(a) A person uses force in relation to another person or property not only when he or she applies force to, but also where he or she causes an impact on, the body of that person or that property
> (b) a person shall be treated as using force in relation to another person if
>   (i) he or she threatens that person with its use, or
>   (ii) he or she detains that person without actually using it; and
> (c) a person shall be treated as using force in relation to property if he or she threatens a person with its use in relation to property."

Section 20(3) goes on to provide that a threat of force may be reasonable although actual use of force may not be.

Where the defendant had an opportunity to retreat before resorting to the use of force, s.20(4) of the Act provides that this is a factor to be taken into account in deciding whether the use of force by the defendant was reasonable. In *R v McInnes* [1971] 3 All E.R. 295, the Court of Appeal held that while there was no absolute duty to retreat at common law, failure to do so could be taken into account in determining the reasonableness of the use of force by the accused. This ruling was approved of in this jurisdiction in *People (AG) v Dwyer* [1972] I.R. 416.

The defences under ss.18 and 19 also apply to acts that are immediately preparatory to the use of force.

22. INFANCY

The defence of Infancy is based on the common law doctrine of *doli incapax* which regards children under a certain age as being incapable of forming *mens rea*. *Doli incapax* simply means "incapable of crime". In this jurisdiction, children are categorised into different age groups for the purposes of criminal liability.

22.1 Children under the age of seven years

A child who is younger than seven years of age is conclusively presumed to be *doli incapax*. This presumption cannot be rebutted, regardless of the actual understanding of the child or the circumstances in which the alleged offence takes place.

22.2 Children between seven and 14 years

Children who are between seven and 14 years of age are presumed to be *doli incapax*. The difference between this group and those in the younger age group is that if the child is older than seven and younger than 14 years of age, the presumption of *doli incapax* may be rebutted where there is evidence of a "mischievous discretion". The standard required to rebut the presumption is quite high and requires that the child knew that his conduct went beyond mere mischief. The test is whether the child appreciated the seriousness of his actions. In *R v Gorrie* (1919) 83 JP 136, the court held that the child had to know that his conduct was gravely or very seriously wrong. This test was followed in this jurisdiction in *KM v DPP* [1994] 1 I.R. 514.

Until the passing of the Criminal Law (Rape) (Amendment) Act 1990, a boy younger than 14 years of age was conclusively presumed to be incapable of committing rape. This presumption applied to the offence of rape only and did not preclude the prosecution of a boy under the age of 14 for other forms of sexual assault. This presumption has been abolished by s.6 of the Criminal Law (Rape) (Amendment) Act 1990 with the result that provided the presumption of *doli incapax* is rebutted, a boy who is aged between seven and 14 years of age can now be charged with rape.

22.3 The Children Act 2001

Part V of the Children Act 2001 deals with Criminal Responsibility and in particular s.52 of the Act raises the age of criminal responsibility to 12 and states that "it shall be conclusively presumed that no child under the age of 12 years is capable of committing an offence". Section 52(2) provides that "there is a rebuttable presumption that a child who is not less than 12 but under 14 years of age is incapable of committing an offence because the child did not have the capacity to know that the act or omission was wrong". These provisions will have the effect of widening the group of children who are conclusively presumed to be *doli incapax* and narrowing the group of children to whom a rebuttable presumption applies. Section 52 of the 2001 Act awaits enforcement by Ministerial Order although most of the other provisions of the 2001 Act are in force. Until that happens, Ireland will continue to have the lowest age of criminal responsibility in Europe.

23. DURESS AND NECESSITY

The defence of duress is available to an accused person who has been charged with an offence other than murder and applies where the accused acted as he did due to threats made against him or a third party. The determining issue here is not whether the accused had formed *mens rea* but rather whether his will was overborne to the point where he could not be blamed for acting as he did.

In *People (AG) v Whelan* [1934] I.R. 518, the accused was charged with receiving stolen property. He stated that threats of extreme violence had compelled him to act as he did. The jury agreed and the matter was referred to the Court of Criminal Appeal, which was asked whether or not, given the finding of the jury, the accused was guilty or innocent of receiving stolen property. The Court of Criminal Appeal held "that threats of immediate death or serious personal violence so great as to overbear the ordinary power of human relations should be accepted as justification for acts which would otherwise be criminal. The application of this general rule must, however, be subject to certain limitations" (*per* Murnaghan J. at 520). The test laid down in *Whelan* appears to be objective, referring as it does to the "ordinary power of human resistance" and not to the power of the accused to resist. The test further requires that the threat should be immediate so that a threat to inflict injury at some future juncture will negative the defence since the accused could hardly argue that his will could be overborne to such an extent by a remote threat.

The duress must not be self-induced. In *R v Shepard* [1987] 86 Cr. App. R. 47, the accused had joined a gang who engaged in shoplifting. When he tried to break free of the gang he was subjected to intimidation. In the circumstances, the court held that the jury should have been given the opportunity to consider the effects of duress on the accused. However, a different conclusion had been reached in *R v Fitzpatrick* [1997] N.I. 20, where the accused had been charged with murder, membership of an unlawful organisation and robbery. In this case, the defence of duress was not accepted and on appeal, it was held that where an accused joins an unlawful organisation voluntarily, he cannot then assert that he was entirely free from moral culpability and as a consequence, cannot rely on the defence of duress.

23.1 Necessity

This defence has certain similarities to that of duress. Like duress, the defence of necessity is not available to an accused charged with murder. In *R v Dudley and Stevens* (1884) Cox CC 624, the two accused were convicted of murder and sentenced to death, although the sentence was later commuted to six months' imprisonment. The defendants had been on a lifeboat for a number of weeks with two others and had killed one of the others and eaten his body. It was accepted that had they not done so, they would all have died. In their defence, it was argued that the deceased would have died anyway and that the defendants had acted out of necessity. The court held however, that a decision such as had been made by the defendants would be one that would be made by the strongest at the expense of the weakest and that it was the function of the law to protect the weak from the strong. The defence arises where prevailing circumstances compel the accused to act in a particular way, and he elects to commit a criminal offence on the basis that it is the lesser of two evils.

In *R v Pommell* [1995] 2 Cr. App. R. 607, the accused had been charged with being in unlawful possession of a firearm. He argued that he had taken the weapon in order to prevent a murder. In this case, it was held that the defence of necessity was available. Section 18 (3)(b) of the Non-Fatal Offences Against the Person Act 1997 provides for the justifiable use of force against a criminal act which occurs where a defence of duress would have been available. Similarly, a defence akin to necessity appears in s.6(2)(c) of the Criminal Justice Act 1991 as amended by s.21 of the Non-Fatal Offences Against the Person Act 1997.

For the defence to succeed, the accused must have no alternative action available to him and must go no further than is necessary to avoid the greater of the two evils. Like the defence of duress, the defence of necessity may not be invoked where the accused brings about the prevailing circumstances. The test has both an objective and a subjective element, both of which must be proven. First, the accused must have committed the offence to avoid the greater evil. This is subjective and hinges on the belief of the accused as to the reasonableness of his conduct. Secondly, the actions of the accused must be what a reasonable person with the characteristics of the accused would have done in the same situation. Where one of these aspects is absent, the defence will fail.

24. MISTAKE

There is no general defence of mistake *per se*, but the law recognises that there may be situations in which the accused ought not to be convicted of an offence where he acted under a mistaken belief as to the facts of his situation. The Latin maxim *ignorantia facti excusat; ignorantia juris non excusat* encapsulates the general rule that a mistake of fact will be excused whereas a mistake of law will not. Where an accused acts under a mistake of the law, he will be liable for his conduct. In *People (DPP) v Healy* [1990] 1 I.L.R.M. 313, the court stated that to allow an accused to be absolved of liability on the basis that he had made a mistake of law would be "to put a premium on ignorance". There are some exceptions to the general rule that a mistake of law will not excuse an accused. An example of this can be seen in s.4 of the Criminal Justice (Theft and Fraud Offences) Act 2001. Theft, under s.4 of the 2001 Act, occurs when the accused "dishonestly" appropriates property without the consent of the owner and with the intention of depriving the owner of the property. "Dishonesty" is defined in the Act as being "without a claim of right made in good faith".

At common law, an unreasonable mistake would not absolve an accused of liability for his conduct. In *R v Tolson* (1889) 23 QBD 706, the accused married a man believing that her husband was dead and was charged with bigamy when it transpired some years later that her husband was in fact alive. She was acquitted on the basis that she had made a reasonable mistake. In *DPP v Morgan* [1975] 2 All E.R. 347, the House of Lords held that a genuinely held belief, regardless of how unreasonable it might have been, meant that the defendants could not have formed the *mens rea* for the offence with which they were charged, which in their case was rape. In *R v Kimber* [1983] 3 All E.R. 316, it was held that a genuine mistake of fact could lead to an acquittal in cases other than rape. The accused will in most cases be judged according to his mistaken belief but the court must have regard to the presence or absence of reasonable grounds for the belief. Mistake of fact will not always lead to an acquittal. Where an offence is one of absolute liability, mistake is irrelevant since no *mens rea* is required, proof of *actus reus* being sufficient to impose liability.

25. CONSENT

Whether consent is a defence to a criminal charge depends on the nature of the charge and the capacity of the person from whom consent is sought, to give consent. The *actus reus* of some offences such as assault and theft involves the absence of consent and in these situations, the presence of consent will be a defence. Consent is irrelevant for other offences. An accused charged with an offence under s.2 of the Criminal Law (Sexual Offences) Act 2006 will be convicted notwithstanding the fact that the person with whom he had sexual intercourse purported to consent to it, unless he had genuinely believed that the person was over the age of consent. Equally, an accused who ends another person's life, even at that other person's request and with their consent, will still be convicted of murder.

26. PREPARING FOR A CRIMINAL LAW EXAM

The prospect of any examination can be a daunting one and that is particularly true in the case of examinations in law. The sheer breadth of content in any given area of law is such that it is virtually impossible to cover every single topic in great detail. Nonetheless, the student who engages in "topic spotting" runs a very high risk of being caught short. It is therefore not advisable to cover the minimum number of subject areas in the hope that they will appear on an exam paper. That is not to say that certain topics don't show up year after year. Students should have regard to past papers, but only as a guideline. However tempting it may be to hedge one's bets and prepare answers in advance of an exam, it is a temptation that is best avoided.

26.1 BEFORE THE EXAM

Don't leave it until the last minute to familiarise yourself with the library facilities. Every student knows that there will be an exam at some point whether at the end of a semester or at the end of the academic year and should make sure that they have all the relevant materials that will be needed to prepare for the exam. Reading lists are usually provided at the beginning of a course and it is better to work your way through it over the course of the year than to leave it until a couple of weeks before the exam. Where reading lists say that some texts are essential, priority should be given to using these. Other readings are recommended and should, where possible, also be consulted. For a law student, textbooks are only one essential source of information; it is not possible to study law without familiarising yourself with the cases that are relevant to whatever area of law you are studying. To that end, the sooner a student comes to terms with reading the judgments of the courts, the better. Reading case law is not an activity that you will be giving up any time soon if you go into practice. As well as textbooks and cases, students should be familiar with the relevant legislation in a given area. Statutes are available online and may be downloaded from the website of the Irish Government: www.irlgov.ie Students should also make use of the various legal journals and be familiar with various reports. The Reports and Consultation Papers of the Law Reform Commission of

Ireland are particularly important since they have often formed the basis for legislative reform in many areas of law.

26.2 THE EXAM

An exam in law usually consists of two different types of question: the essay style question and the problem question. Many students have difficulty in answering the latter and mistakenly believe that the former is an open invitation to write all they know about the subject of the essay. This is one time where subjective belief will not be of assistance. If you are asked to attempt four questions from a choice of eight, do not make the mistake of spending a disproportionate amount of time on any one question. One brilliantly answered question will not result in a very high grade if all the other questions are only half-answered. It is very important to bear this in mind and to spend roughly the same amount of time on all questions. Leave some space at the end of each question so that you can return to it if you wish to add anything to your answer. Do not waste your time re-writing the question from the exam paper; simply indicate which question you are attempting. If you've made a mistake, cross it out. Try and keep your handwriting legible and use appropriate terminology—using numbers and other forms of shorthand instead of letters should be confined to text messaging. Finally, and perhaps most importantly, read the question and answer it—do not answer the question you hoped you'd been asked. If you have any questions about the instructions contained on the exam paper or if you can't understand a particular question, alert the attention of the invigilator and seek clarification.

26.3 ESSAY QUESTIONS

An essay question will normally begin with some proposition which the student is asked to "critically analyse" or "critically evaluate" or "discuss". An essay question will never ask the student to write all they know about the topic in question. To answer an essay question properly, the student must appreciate what precisely is being asked. A student should address the issue raised in the question and outline this in the first part of their answer. The answer should then focus on the law in relation to the issue in question using references from cases, legislation, academic authorities and relevant reports. Comparison should be made between this jurisdiction and others in terms of how the issue has arisen and/or been dealt with. Finally, the student should draw together the points made to form some conclusion and perhaps suggest how the issue might be resolved or if the issue involves a change in the law. The essay type question shows the examiner a number of things such as:

- The student's ability to address a specific issue.
- The student's ability to analyse and summarise the key points raised.
- Breadth and depth of reading.
- Knowledge of the law.
- The student's ability to cogently argue a point.
- The student's ability to recognise what points are relevant to the discussion.

An essay should be well structured with a beginning, middle and a conclusion.

26.4 PROBLEM QUESTIONS

These questions are often felt by students to be more difficult than essay questions. The reason for this presumably is that students will have been more used to writing essays at school. Problem questions usually begin with a factual scenario and conclude with the request to "advise" someone. In many cases (but not always), the factual scenarios provided will closely resemble a well-known case. It is crucial to read these questions more than once with a view to ascertaining what issues must be dealt with. There are usually a number of legal issues that arise from the facts given and insofar as they relate to the person to be advised, must be dealt with. Where the student is asked to advise more than one person, it is usually best to deal with them separately. Sometimes the issue will be identified for you—for example, you might be given a factual scenario and asked to "Advise Joe Bloggs on his liability under the Non-Fatal Offences Against the Person Act 1997." In that case, you will need to identify the offences under that Act with which Joe might be charged. What are the elements of those offences? Does Joe have any defences available to him? It is more common however, to simply be asked to "advise" in general terms. The best way to answer problem questions is to be methodical. If you are permitted to bring a piece of legislation into the exam with you, do not spend time re-writing the provisions contained within it—simply refer to the relevant section and say what it provides for. It is not necessary to give full citations of cases and do not waste time telling the examiner the facts of the case. Simply state what point of law the case established or what proposition the case is authority for. Students should only give brief facts about cases if they can't remember the name of the case.

Step 1
- Identify the legal issues arising from the facts given. Do not confuse issues of law with issues of fact. If, for example, you are told that Joe is 26 years of age, that is a matter of fact, not of law, since Joe's age is irrelevant to the legal issues. If, however, you are told that Joe is six years of age, this is a relevant legal issue (as well as being a fact), since the doctrine of *doli incapax* will provide Joe with an absolute defence.

Step 2
- Identify the relevant law. What statute(s) or common law rule(s) govern the issues? Which cases are relevant?
- Which offences might have been committed? What are the elements of those offences? Bear in mind that a number of offences might be relevant or that the conduct engaged in may be criminalised under different pieces of legislation.
- What defences are disclosed by the facts of the situation?

Step 3
- Apply the law to Joe's situation by answering the following:
  – What conduct has Joe engaged in? With what offences might he be charged? What defences are disclosed by the facts of the situation?
  – Does any conduct on Joe's part deny him any such defence?
  – What must be established in order to fix Joe with liability for his act or omission?

Step 4
- Advise Joe by telling him the strengths and weaknesses of his case and on the likely penalties on conviction.

26.5 After the Exam

Do not engage in post mortem examinations of the exam. It will do nothing to help you prepare for your next exam and you have no reason to believe that the person you are talking to has done any better than you have. Once you've handed up your paper, leave it and move on.

INDEX

Abduction, child, 74
Absolute liability
   mens rea, 35, 45
   mistake, 137
Actus reus
   affray, 91
   assault, 64, 65–66, 92, 93
   attempts, 101–102
   burglary, 81, 83
   causing serious harm, 66
   coincidence with *mens rea*, 35
      continuing acts, 35–36
      duty to mitigate, 36
      "supposed corpse rule", 36
   conspiracy, 103
   disorderly conduct, 87
   element of a crime, 27
   false imprisonment, 73
   incitement, 104
   intoxication in public place, 86
   meaning, 28
      omissions, 29–30, 50–51
      state of affairs, 28–29
      voluntary actions, 30
   obscene displays, 88
   property
      damaging, 76, 77
      stolen, 84
   riot, 90
   robbery, 83
   secondary parties, 41
   syringe offences, 68, 69
   theft, 79
   threatening/abusive/insulting behaviour, 87
   threats to kill/cause serious harm, 67
   violent disorder, 90
   wilful obstruction, 88, 93
Affray, 91

Aiding and abetting, 39, 40
Arrest and detention
   habeas corpus, 16
   powers of, 14–15, 100
   rights on, 15–16
Arrestable offences
   definition, 3
Arson, 77
Assault, 64–65
Assault, aggravated sexual, 58–59
Assault, sexual, 57–58
Assault causing harm, 65–66
   see also Causing serious harm
Assault of a Garda, 92–93
Assault with intent, 91–92
Attempts, 37, 48, 101–103
Automatism
   basic/specific intent crime, 120–121
   definition, 118
   generally, 118
   internal/external factors, 118–119
   self-induced, 119–121

Bail
   generally, 17
   grounds for refusal
      Bail Act 1997, 21
      Bunreacht na hÉireann, 20–21
      case law, 18–20
      hearsay evidence, 23
      jurisdiction to grant, 17–18
      sentencing, 22–23
Basic intent crimes, 114–115, 117, 120–121
Bunreacht na hÉireann
   bail, 20–21
   impact of, 4–7
   source of law, 3

Burden of proof, 2, 27, 125
Burglary, 81–82
   aggravated, 82–83
   entry, 82
   trespass, 82

Causation
   novus actus interveniens, 37–38
      eggshell skull rule, 38
   result offences, 36–37, 48
Causing serious harm, 66
   threats, 67
Central Criminal/High Court, 5, 10–11
Children
   abduction, 74
   doli incapax, 2, 133–134
   infanticide, 51
   sexual offences, 59–60, 61–62
Circuit Court, 10
Coercion, 71
   see also Duress
Common design, 42–44
Computers
   "hacking", 78
   unlawful use of, 81
Consent
   assault, 64–65
      aggravated sexual, 58–59
      sexual, 57
   causing serious harm, 58–59, 66–67
   damage to property, 75
   euthanasia, 52
   false imprisonment, 73–74
   generally, 138
   incest, 62
   rape, 54–56, 57
      statutory, 59
   theft, 79–80
Conspiracy, 103–104
Corporate liability, 45–46
   see also Vicarious liability

Counselling and procuring, 39, 40–41
Courts
   Circuit, 10
   Criminal Appeal, 11–12
   District, 9–10
   High/Central Criminal, 5, 10–11
   Special Criminal, 11
   Supreme, 4, 5, 13, 16
      unconstitutional laws, 53
Criminal Assets Bureau, 25
Criminal offence, elements of
   actus reus
      generally, 27, 28
      omissions, 29–30, 50–51
      state of affairs, 28–29
      voluntary actions, 30
   coincidence of *actus reus* and *mens rea*, 35–36
   mens rea
      criminal negligence, 34–35, 50
      generally, 27, 30
      intention, 30–32
      presumption of intent, 32–33
      recklessness, 33–34, 56
   novus actus interveniens, 37–38
   proof, 2, 27–28, 125
   see also *actus reus*; *mens rea*

Damaging property, 75–76
   with intent to defraud, 76–77
   with intent to endanger life, 76
   possession with intent to damage, 78
   threats to damage, 77
   see also property offences
Deception, 80–81
Defences
   automatism
      basic/specific intent crime, 120–121
      definition, 118

Index

Defences—cont'd
  automatism—cont'd
    generally, 118
    internal/external factors, 118–119
    self-induced, 119–121
  consent
    assault, 64–65
    assault, aggravated sexual, 58–59
    assault, sexual, 57
    causing serious harm, 58–59, 66–67
    damage to property, 75
    euthanasia, 52
    false imprisonment, 73–74
    generally, 138
    incest, 62
    rape, 54–56, 57
    rape, statutory, 59
    theft, 79–80
  duress, 135
  infancy, 2, 133–134
  insanity
    appeals, 124
    burden of proof, 125
    consequences of plea, 129
    diminished responsibility, 124
    fitness to be tried, 122–123
    generally, 122
    irresistible impulse, 128–129
    M'Naghten rules, 125–127
    Review Board, 124
    section 5 verdict, 123
  intoxication
    basic/specific intent crime, 114–115, 117
    capacity to form *mens rea*, 114–117
    Dutch courage, 116
    generally, 114
    Irish law, 116–117
    voluntary/involuntary, 115–116

Defences—cont'd
  introduction, 107
  mistake, 35, 59–60, 137
  necessity, 136
  provocation
    common law, 108–109
    conduct, 111–112
    cumulative, 111
    Irish law, 109–112
    proportionality, 112
  self-defence
    excessive, 112–113
    force, 132
    generally, 130
    justifiable use of force, 130–132
  see also Impossibility
Demands for payment, 72
Detention *see* Arrest and detention
Disorder, violent, 90
Disorderly conduct, 86–87
District Court, 9–10
Doli incapax, 2, 133–134
Drunkenness, 114
  see also Intoxication
Duress, 135
  see also Coercion

Eggshell skull rule, 38
Endangerment, 73
European Court of Human Rights, 8, 59, 61
Euthanasia, 52

False accounting, 81
False imprisonment, 73–74
Function of criminal law, 1–2

Habeas corpus, 16
"Hacking", 78
Harassment, 71–72
Hearsay evidence
  objection to bail, 23

High/Criminal Central Court, 5, 10–11
Homicide
   euthanasia, 52
   infanticide, 51
   manslaughter
     breach of duty, 50–51
     criminal and dangerous act, 49–50
     criminal negligence, 34–35, 50
     voluntary/involuntary, 49
   murder
     aggravated, 48–49
     attempted, 48
     causation, 36–38, 48
     definition, 47–48

Impossibility
   attempts, 102–103
   conspiracy, 104
   incitement, 105
Incest, 42, 62–63
Inchoate offences
   attempts, 37
     actus reus and proximity, 101–102
     impossibility, 102–103
     mens rea, 48, 102
   conspiracy, 103
     impossibility, 104
   generally, 40, 101
   incitement
     case law, 104–105
     impossibility, 105
     statutory, 106
Incitement, 104–106
Indictable offences
   jurisdiction of courts, 3–4, 10
Infancy
   under 7 years, 2, 133
   between 7 and 14 years, 2, 133
   changes under Children Act 2001, 134
   see also Children

Infanticide, 51
Insanity
   appeals, 124
   burden of proof, 125
   consequences of plea, 129
   diminished responsibility, 124
   fitness to be tried, 122–123
   generally, 122
   irresistible impulse, 128–129
   M'Naghten rules, 125–127
   Review Board, 124
   section 5 verdict, 123
Intention
   direct intent, 30
   oblique intent, 30–32
   presumption of intent, 32–33
Intoxication
   capacity to form *mens rea*, 114–117
   in a public place, 86

Joint enterprise, 42–44
Judicial review
   constitutionality of laws, 4, 5, 7, 53
   decisions of DPP, 11

Manslaughter
   breach of duty, 50–51
   criminal and dangerous act, 49–50
   criminal negligence, 34–35, 50
   voluntary/involuntary, 49
Mens rea
   absolute liability, 35, 45
   affray, 91
   aggravated sexual assault, 58
   assault, 64, 66, 92, 93
   attempts, 48, 102
   burglary, 81–82, 83
   causing serious harm, 66
   coincidence with *actus reus*, 35
     continuing acts, 35–36
     duty to mitigate, 36

Index

Mens rea—cont'd
  coincidence with *actus reus*
    —cont'd
      "supposed corpse rule", 36
  conspiracy, 103
  criminal negligence, 34–35, 50
  disorderly conduct, 87
  doli incapax, 2, 133–134
  element of a crime, 27
  generally, 27, 30
  incitement, 105
  intention, 30
    direct, 30
    oblique, 30–32
  intoxication
    capacity to form, 114–117
    in a public place, 86
  manslaughter
    voluntary/involuntary, 49
  mistake, 137
  murder, 47
  obscene displays, 88
  presumption of intent, 32–33
  property
    damaging, 76, 77
    stolen, 84
  rape, 56, 57
  recklessness, 33–34, 56
  riot, 90
  robbery, 83
  secondary parties, 41–42
  strict liability, 35, 44
  syringe offences, 68, 69, 70
  theft, 79
  threatening/abusive/insulting behaviour, 87
  threats to kill/cause serious harm, 67
  transferred intent, 46, 69
  violent disorder, 90
  wilful obstruction, 88, 93
Mentally ill persons
  sexual offences against, 60–61

Miscarriages of justice, 12
Mistake, 35, 59–60, 137
Motive, 30
Murder
  aggravated, 48–49
  attempted, 48
  causation, 36-38, 48
  definition, 47–48

Necessity, 136
Negligence, criminal, 34–35, 50
Novus actus interveniens, 37–38
  eggshell skull rule, 38

Obscene displays, 88
Obstruction
  endangering traffic, 73
  wilful, 88–89
    of a Peace Officer, 92–93
Offences
  arrestable, 3
  "either way", 4, 9–10
  indictable, 3–4, 10
  summary, 3–4, 9
Offences Against the State Acts 1939–1998
  detention period, 15, 100
  failure to answer, 98, 99
  generally, 96
  Special Criminal Court, 11
  Suppression Orders, 97–98
  unlawful organisations, 96–97
    directing, 99–100
    membership of, 98–99
Offensive conduct, 87
Official Secrets Act 1963, 95–96
Omissions, 29–30, 50–51

Parties
  common design, 42–44
  corporations, 45–46
  participation by omissions, 29–30, 50–51

Parties—cont'd
  secondary, 39–42
  vicarious liability, 44
  victims, 26, 42
Poisoning, 72–73
Proof
  burden of, 2, 27, 125
  standard of, 2, 27–28, 125
Property offences
  arson, 77
  burglary, 81–82
    aggravated, 82–83
    entry, 82
    trespass, 82
  damaging, 75–76
  damaging with intent to defraud, 76–77
  damaging with intent to endanger life, 76
  deception, 80–81
  false accounting, 81
  possession with intent to damage, 78
  robbery, 83–84
  stolen property
    handling, 84
    possession, 84–85
  theft, 78–79
    consent, 79-80
    dishonesty, 79
    property defined, 80
  threats to damage, 77
  unauthorised accessing of data, 78
  unlawful use of a computer, 81
Provocation
  common law, 108–109
  conduct, 111–112
  cumulative, 111
  Irish law, 109–112
  proportionality, 112
Public order offences
  affray, 91

Public order offences—cont'd
  assault with intent, 91–92
  assault or obstruction of a Garda, 92–93
  disorderly conduct, 86–87
  enforcement powers, 89
  intoxication, 86
  obscene displays, 88
  offensive conduct, 87
  riot, 89–90
  threatening/abusive/insulting behaviour, 87–88
  violent disorder, 90
  wilful obstruction, 88–89
    of a Peace Officer, 92–93
Punishment
  community service orders, 25
  compensation, 26
  fines, 25
  forfeiture, 25–26
  imprisonment, 24
  probation, 26

Rape
  "common law", 54
    consent, 54–56
    mens rea, 56
  statutory, 59–60
  under 1990 Act, 57
Recklessness
  meaning, 33–34, 56
"Right to die", 52
Riot, 89–90
Robbery, 83–84

Secondary participation
  actus reus, 41
  aiding and abetting, 39, 40
  compared to common design, 42
  counselling, 39, 40–41
  mens rea, 41–42
  procuring, 39, 41
Sedition, 94–95

Index

Self-defence, 130–132
   excessive, 112–113
Sentencing
   mandatory/discretionary, 24
   offences while on bail, 22–23
Sex Offenders Act 2001, 63
Sexual offences
   background and changes, 53
   between males, 61–62
   gross indecency, 62
   incest, 42, 62–63
   mentally ill persons, 60–61
   rape, "common law", 54
      consent, 54–56
      mens rea, 56
   rape, statutory, 59–60
   rape under 1990 Act, 57
   Sex Offenders Act 2001, 63
   sexual assault, 57–58
      aggravated, 58–59
Sources of law
   Bunreacht na hÉireann, 3, 4–7
   common law, 3
   European Convention on Human Rights, 8
   European Convention on Human Rights Act 2003, 8
   statute, 3
Special Criminal Court, 11
Specific intent crimes, 114–115, 117, 120–121
"Spiking" drinks, 72–73
"Stalking", 71–72
Standard of proof, 2, 27–28, 125
State, offences against
   Offences Against the State Acts 1939–98, 15, 96–100
   Official Secrets Act 1963, 95–96

State, offences against—cont'd
   sedition, 94–95
   treason, 94
Stolen property, 84–85
Strict liability
   mens rea, 35, 44
Suicide, 47, 52
Summary offences
   jurisdiction of courts, 3–4, 9
Supreme Court
   appeal to, 5, 13, 16
   refer Bills to, 4
   unconstitutional laws, 53
Syringe offences
   attacks, 68
   definitions, 68
   possession and abandonment, 70–71
   spraying blood/blood-like substance, 69
   stabbing, 69–70

Theft, 78–79
   consent, 79–80
   dishonesty, 79
   property defined, 80
Threatening/abusive/insulting behaviour, 87–88
Threats
   damage property, 77
   kill/cause serious harm, 67
Transferred intent, 46, 69
Treason, 94

Vicarious liability, 44
Victims of crime
   compensation, 26
   not accessories, 42
Violent disorder, 90